THE STORY OF LINDBERGH
THE LONE EAGLE

THE "LONE EAGLE" AND HIS MOTHER

The first man to fly from New York to Paris, and his mother, Mrs. Evangeline L. Lindbergh, taken before the start of the historic flight. In the background is the transatlantic plane.

THE STORY OF
LINDBERGH
THE LONE EAGLE

INCLUDING

THE DEVELOPMENT OF AVIATION, EPOCH-MAKING
FLIGHTS OF THE WORLD'S GREATEST AIRMEN, AND
THE HISTORY OF EFFORTS TO BRIDGE THE DIS-
TANCE BETWEEN THE OLD AND NEW WORLDS

By
RICHARD J. BEAMISH
MEMBER AËRO CLUB OF PENNSYLVANIA
AUTHOR AMERICA'S PART IN THE WORLD WAR

𝔍𝔩𝔩𝔲𝔰𝔱𝔯𝔞𝔱𝔢𝔡

1927
PRINTED IN THE U. S. A. AT
THE INTERNATIONAL PRESS

FOREWORD

SINCE time began upon the earth, human beings have walked or ridden upon the land or have floated in one form or another upon the waters. Not until the Wright Brothers blazed the way for aviation was there any real progress in the conquest of the air.

Human fears were at the root of that long hesitancy in attempting flight. The shuddering fear with which most persons looked down from great heights, the nightmare that wakes us trembling as we dream of falling through infinite space; these are familiar forms of the earthbound terrors that have lain in the roots of our being.

It was inevitable that the spirit of man should some day rise above his fears and rule the empyrean in which for countless ages the eagles have been emperors. To one man has come the glory of showing the way to that mystery. Charles Augustus Lindbergh, a twenty-five-year-old mail pilot of the United States, by his lonely flight from Roosevelt Field, just outside of New York, to Le Bourget, the airport of Paris, has shown what one man may daringly achieve.

The spiritual stature of this young American is revealed in the modesty with which he identifies himself with the *Spirit of St. Louis* in which he made this epic flight. "We," he says, in speaking of that magnificent adventure. He and his Ryan monoplane

and his Wright whirlwind motor were partners.
Sturdy, staunch, well-tested, and enduring, these three
companions in the most dangerous flight ever made
by one man.

The same clear-visioned truth and modesty that
impelled him to acknowledge companionship and
credit with his inanimate ship and motor brought him
with high credit through the greatest series of ovations
that have ever been given to one man.

France honored him as she has honored no one since
Napoleon. Belgium through its King and Queen
gave to him royal honor. England through its King
and Queen and the magnetic Prince of Wales was at
his feet. Last of all, our own America, from pauper
to millionaire, rose up with mighty acclaim to welcome
him home.

Through all of this, Lindbergh, the Lone Eagle, has
remained himself, truest type of American manhood.

This story of his achievement is published with the
hope that his magnificent example will fashion the
American of tomorrow in the image of his superb spirit.

CONTENTS

CONTENTS

CONTENTS

CONTENTS

CONTENTS

CHAPTER I

The Flight of the Lone Eagle

A LEAN, tanned face smiled from a closed airplane cabin at a cheering crowd. A long, strong, young hand flipped good-by at the receding earth. The tanned face wiped out the smile and reset its lines in serious determination. A long, gray, man-made bird, that seemed to be the visible symbol of the gallant soul in its tiny cabin, rushed heavily down along the runway.

Heavily it lifted and jerked upward from a spot of earth softened by the rain that a few hours before had come from low-lying clouds. The crowd watched breathlessly. Would the great *Spirit of St. Louis* lift its load of 448 gallons of gasoline and 28 gallons of oil, 5150 pounds in all, in addition to its own dead weight and that of the gallant man at its controls?

Three times on the rush from the 3800 feet of the runway the plane struck soft spots and leaped for all the world like an aged and corpulent frog! Once it escaped by only a few inches a collision with a road scraper as its nose turned slowly upward toward the clouds. It had come almost to the edge of the runway where perilous ditches lay in wait when it finally shook itself free from the earth and rose steadily and slowly on its epoch-making journey. At the very last as it was leaving Roosevelt Flying Field, it barely cleared a network of telephone and telegraph wires. As it climbed to safety, the morning mist was lifted like the curtain of a great theater and the thousands on the field below felt their breaths and their pulses resume their normal ebb and flow.

"I didn't think he'd make it," said Clarence D. Chamberlin, who two weeks later piloted a Bellanca plane to Germany. "It seemed to me he was just holding that plane up in the air by his own will power. It was a beautiful take-off and the way it was accomplished was a miracle."

That brave, miraculous start told in miniature the story of the world's greatest flight and the character of the modest, brave, young American who made it. Captain Charles Augustus Lindbergh, (now Colonel Lindbergh), in the days that were to come, always said "we" when he described that flight. To him the *Spirit of St. Louis* was part of himself; a twinned creature in the performance of the bravest and most skilful single performance ever accomplished by man.

He had talked of the flight from New York to Paris as cheerfully and almost as casually as an ordinary person who goes on a day's journey by rail. His widowed mother, Mrs. Evangeline Land Lindbergh, as wonderful in her quiet courage as her tall, blithe son, had journeyed to New York several days before to wish him Godspeed and kiss him good-by, and had then returned to her classroom in the Cass Technical High School of Detroit where she taught chemistry. His granduncle, John C. Lodge, chairman of Detroit's Council and Acting Mayor, in an interview had told of his absolute confidence that his nephew would make the flight. "From childhood he has been fear-blind. In

THE "SPIRIT OF ST. LOUIS"

Lindbergh's plane on the first leg of the transatlantic flight. The famous identification number N-X-211 can be seen on the wing.

IN FLYING TOGS

Captain Lindbergh in flying clothes at Curtiss Field a few days
before the takeoff.

addition he has determination, great skill, and the self-confidence that comes to natural leaders. He has belief in himself and has mapped out his own course since he was eight years old."

The clouds had made a gray canopy for days over Roosevelt Field near Garden City, L. I. Three airplanes had been made ready for a transatlantic flight when the weather should have made navigation and flight possible. Lieutenant Commander Richard E. Byrd, of the United States Navy, the first flier to cross the North Pole in an airplane, was ready with the triple-engined Fokker, *America*. His expedition, which was to include several besides himself, had been financed by Rodman Wanamaker, a merchant prince of Philadelphia and New York. The Bellanca plane, *Columbia*, which had established a world's record nonstop flight, was also waiting in its hangar. Like the *America*, it was to carry more than one. Only the little Ryan monoplane, the *Spirit of St. Louis*, was a solo plane.

EAGER FOR ACTION

When darkness fell on the night of Thursday, May 19, rain dripped from the low clouds and spiteful gusts came from the northeast fitfully. It was impossible flying weather.

Lindbergh ate his dinner as usual with the other fliers in the Garden City Hotel. After dinner he walked around the hotel grounds and studied the weather. At eleven o'clock it was still bad, and he went to bed, leaving instructions to awaken him if the wind died and the clouds lifted. Government reports on the weather were coming in hourly to the little group quartered in the hotel.

The twelve o'clock survey overhead showed clearing skies, and the report from Washington indicated that Friday would bring fair weather all along the Atlantic Coast. At one o'clock the indications were even better. At two o'clock, after a brief conference of Lindbergh's friends, chief among them B. F. Mahoney, the president of the Ryan Air Lines, it was decided to awaken the flier.

He had been asleep a little less than three hours, but he snapped out of a deep and untroubled slumber, eager and wide-eyed in an instant. The call had come and he was ready. Hastily he donned the riding breeches and khaki shirt, the army socks and the heavy tan shoes that he was not to lay aside until he had arrived in the heart of fashionable Paris. Mr. Mahoney's car was waiting and without fuss or flurry, they whirled off to the hangar.

Instantly the "grapevine telegraph," that mysterious communication by which newspaper men and the observers of the Army and Navy learn that important things are about to happen, commenced to work. Roosevelt Field was the honey pot that drew a throng of curious human flies. Inside Lindbergh's hangar the lights were snapped on as he and a corps of mechanics made the final inspection inch by inch, inside and outside, of the beautiful plane.

"LET'S GO!"

G. M. Stumpf, representative of the St. Louis Chamber of Commerce which sponsored the flight, entered, rubbing his sleepy eyes. Lindbergh looked at him and smiled. "Let's go!" he said. At his nod the mechanics commenced to fill the big tanks of his plane. They kept on pouring until the gauge registered 448 gallons. This was 145 more gallons than the plane had ever before lifted. "I know she'll rise with it," said Mahoney.

The entrance of the hangar had been roped off, but at a word from Lindbergh or Mahoney, the barrier was lifted from time to time to admit favored persons. Richard E. Byrd was one of these. Then came Bert Acosta, Byrd's pilot, and Lieutenant G. O. Noville, who was also booked for the flight on the *America*. Clarence Chamberlin, pilot of the waiting Bellanca, Raymond Orteig, Jr., and Jean Orteig, sons of Raymond Orteig who had offered the $25,000 prize for the first successful flight between New York and Paris, were also admitted.

FUEL AND PROVISIONS

As dawn made a gray smudge upon the horizon, the long and tedious task of inspecting the plane, testing every part, of putting in the oil and gasoline, came to an end.

Mahoney, who had been walking in and out of the hangar anxiously, like a mother hen hovering over a favorite chick, brought in a package of sandwiches. Two of these were of ham, two of roast beef, and one of hard-boiled eggs. "These are enough," said Lindbergh, taking the two of ham and two of roast beef. "Take this one too, you may need it," said Mahoney. "Oh, pshaw!" replied the flier. "I have enough here for a week."

"You do what I tell you!" commanded Mahoney, as he placed the egg sandwich with the others.

In another nook of the plane was tucked a packet of United States Army emergency rations. These were in tin cans containing fifty-six ounces of dried beef, hardtack, chocolate with dried whites of eggs, and a flavor of caffeine, the acting principle of coffee. The cans were sealed with lead tabs which might easily be pulled off. Enough condensed food was in the packet to last seven days.

PREPARED TO FISH, IF NECESSARY

In still another small packet was a long, strong, linen fish line and four sturdy fishhooks. Like Coli, the Frenchman, who had flown from Paris toward America, with Nungesser, Lindbergh had made preparation for catching his food if by any mischance he was forced down on the ocean or into the wilds of Newfoundland. Another precaution was shown in the heavy-bladed, keen knife carried in the pocket. It was his purpose to use this to hack off crosspieces of his plane and a piece of canvas large enough to make a kite. A seaman's strong needle and heavy thread were in one corner of his pocket and a large ball of heavy twine was in a niche of his ship to use in flying the kite should need come. He walked around his plane and tried the doors and windows of the cabin.

THE LAST PRECAUTION

The last precaution against possible accident was the package of four lifeboat flares safely guarded against the dampness of the air and the possible inrush of sea water by their casings of bicycle inner tubing. Lindbergh's reliance in the event of a forced descent upon the surface of the sea was a pneumatic raft packed in the plane which would enable him to stay afloat several days.

Everything else he needed was on the instrument board before him. There was his clock and the gauges of oil and gasoline, measures that told his height, his speed, and above everything else, the new invention that was to guide him truly over the trackless air, his earth-inductor compass.

A last provision for sustenance was made when two aluminum canteens filled with four quarts of water were hung beside the pilot's wicker seat.

"Are you taking enough food and water?" asked Frank Tichenor, editor of *The Aero Digest*.

"Sure," said Lindbergh, with a grin. "If I get to Paris, I won't need any more, and if I don't get there, I won't need any more either."

His fur-lined, one-piece flying suit was handed to him. He pushed back the helmet and pulled up the flying goggles high on his forehead. With a last, long, searching look at the clouds, he stepped into the closed cabin. Behind the glass that inclosed him, his eager young face could be clearly seen. He rested at ease. His whole frame relaxed, his head leaning forward for a last survey of the dials on his instrument board.

The motor was turned over and he commenced to warm it up. Gently he idled it for a while without opening it up and let it roar. It was necessary that he should get the maximum of power at the beginning of the trip.   The load the Wright whirlwind motor was called upon to lift was the heaviest ever raised by a 200-horsepower engine.   Edward J. Mulligan, field engineer for the Wright Company, stood beside the plane as it throbbed and shook with the violence of power still held in check.

"How is she?" yelled Lindbergh, above the uproar.

"She sounds good to me," shrieked Mulligan.

"Well, then, I might as well go," said the flier.

Mahoney nodded and the mechanics pulled away the blocks from the wheels.   Lindbergh flipped his hand at the crowd.

"So long," he called, just as any American boy might say good-by on a little journey.

THE MOMENT OF DEPARTURE

It was exactly 7.52, Daylight-saving time, when the wheels of the heavily loaded plane started down the runway.   Full daylight had come but great, eager clouds in the east held more than a hint of foreboding. Hundreds of cameras, both moving and still, whirred and clicked, their whirrings and clickings submerged by the roar of Lindbergh's plane.

Down the runway the great plane sped.   It was do or die literally with Lindbergh.   If he failed to lift the tremendous load with that little roaring motor, the chances were that it would pile up in a ditch and immediately burst into flames.

He willed it to lift.   Determination made granite the gay, young face as he gave it the gun.   To the uttermost limit he opened the throttle.

"Up!" his will commanded.   "Up!"

FATHER AND SON

Congressman Charles A. Lindbergh and Colonel Charles A.
Lindbergh at the age of eight.

Photo by *Underwood & Underwood, N. Y.*

THE "SPIRIT OF ST. LOUIS" IN FLIGHT

An inspiring view of the graceful plane in a trial flight over San Diego, California. Captain Lindbergh flew the plane from here to St. Louis in one hop of 2185 miles, breaking all speed records.

Slowly, like a deadened thing suddenly roused into life, it obeyed.   Up it came and then settled as though weary of its task.

"Up!" commanded the soul of Lindbergh and up came the *Spirit of St. Louis*, slowly, steadily, grandly.

Throats of those in the crowd went dry.   Many found it difficult to breathe.   Some felt a sudden rush of tears.

With straining eyes and suffocating lungs they saw the great, gray bird right itself in the air.   They saw it for a few moments outlined dimly against a distant gray cloud.   Slowly, imperceptibly it melted and became part of the cloud.   Lindbergh was on his way.

CHAPTER II

WHILE TWO WORLDS WAITED

A MIRACULOUS mood transformed the whole civilized world when the wheels of the *Spirit of St. Louis* left the earth.

For the first time within the memory of mankind an adventure bringing high rewards was undertaken and no human being envied the adventurer. The minds of humanity in an instant surged and flowed into one great, common ocean in which anxiety and pride were intermingled.

Here was the ultimate and highest daring to which one lone man had ever risen. For the moment Lindbergh was neither American nor Swede. No one thought of the English, Scandinavian, Irish, French, and Canadian bloods that met to make his manhood. He was the soul of man, and in him were the bloods and courages of all the races triumphing over the fears and fetters that have bound humanity from the beginning of time.

So it was that anxiety for his safety became the salt in the ocean of humanity's pride in the great and lonely daring of the Lone Eagle.

Newspaper offices, radio stations, telegraph offices waited tensely for every word telling of his progress. As he passed in turn over Long Island, Massachusetts, Nova Scotia, and finally squared away from the Cape of Newfoundland for his leap over the Atlantic, the news of these successive passages was relayed to those breathlessly waiting in the old and new worlds.

For three hours during Friday afternoon a curtain of static closed down along the Atlantic Coast, making impossible the mere transmission of messages to the great stations along the seacoast. This accident of the ether added to the wide-flung suspense. Would it continue throughout the night and thus handicap efforts to give aid to Lindbergh should he be forced down? That question was asked by thousands.

Fortunately the static lifted and wireless communications were restored shortly before seven o'clock. To every steamship along the Atlantic this message had been relayed:

"Captain Lindbergh in the *Spirit of St. Louis* hopped off for Paris at 7.52 A. M. Summer Time today, May 20th, following Great Circle route. All ships please keep sharp lookout for plane."

Lindbergh was flying without radio equipment. He had sacrificed that safety precaution for the sake of the gasoline supply which replaced it. St. Johns, Newfoundland, reported a heavy fog bank drifting in from the Atlantic and that news made heavy hearted thousands who had hoped for clear weather. They realized how greatly that cold cloud bank added to Lindbergh's handicap. Could they have known of the sleet storm with which the Lone Eagle was battling, their fears would have been increased a thousandfold.

All through the night the watchers in the newspaper offices, the radio stations, and the telegraph offices

watched and waited.   Some ship, they reasoned,
might have seen the *Spirit of St. Louis* like a great,
gray bird winging its lonesome way over the Great
Circle.   Perhaps some whaling ship or coast guard
vessel along the lanes where icebergs floated like great
white sentinels might have spied the intrepid airman.
The hope was in vain.   The long night dragged and no
word came.

THE ODDS TOO GREAT FOR LLOYDS

Newspapers on Saturday morning were messengers
of mingled hope and foreboding.   Nothing definite
was told of the flier's progress.   Rumors were invented but no real information; no ships had sighted
him; no hint of his whereabouts since he had passed
over St. Johns, Newfoundland, had come to the waiting
millions.   Saturday's newspapers printed the story that
Lloyds, the great London agency that will quote
insurance and gambling odds on anything in the
world, had flatly refused to make any quotations on
Lindbergh's chances to reach France.   To many that
little news appeared tragically significant.

Americans along the Atlantic seaboard were getting
ready for the day's business when the first flash of real
relief came.   The Canadian Government wireless
station at Cape Race, Newfoundland, sent broadcast
this message:

"Steamship *Milvesum* from Rotterdam, Holland,
broadcast at 12.10 G.M.T. (8.10 Eastern Daylight
Time) as follows: Lindbergh sighted 500 miles from
Irish Coast.   Plane keeps full speed.   May be expected
8.00 P. M. New York Time in Ireland."

Paris and London received the message from the Dutch steamship at the same time it came to Cape Race. Here was great news. With only five hundred miles to go and a steadily lightening load of fuel, the goal was in sight. The *Spirit of St. Louis* was roaring triumphantly to its appointed goal.

"IS THIS THE WAY TO IRELAND?"

Within a few hours Lindbergh was within three miles of the spot he had marked on the Irish coast, which he had never before seen. As he saw the green mountains he swooped low over an Irish fishing boat and called with all his might, "Is this the way to Ireland?" The roar of the motors carried away the words as the Kerry men in the boat waved excitedly.

And now he was over Dingle Bay. The steam collier *Nogi* sighted and reported the plane shortly before it disappeared over the cliffs of County Kerry on its way to Cork.

And now the suspense was at an end. The great adventure was nearing its triumphal conclusion. The deed that had been dreamed was done. The soul of man had made one more leap upwards toward the infinite.

THE SEARCHLIGHT OF LE BOURGET

It wasn't "Lady Luck" that directed him in his lone flight over the ocean. It was merely a clock, a compass, a collection of maps and charts, well-laid plans, and a mass of knowledge accumulated by long hours of study—these and his own brave spirit carried him over the trackless wastes of the Atlantic to his destined spot on the Irish coast with a precision that was all but uncanny.

As the Lone Eagle sped across Ireland and over England, across the Channel, and into France, the beacons lighted his way. The searchlight of Le Bourget, the most powerful in all the world, shone like a lodestar to show him his way home.

As the *Spirit of St. Louis* dropped noiselessly and lightly into light-flooded Le Bourget, the heart of the world throbbed to a new rhythm.

"Lindbergh has landed!" was the pulse. "Lindbergh has landed!"

CHAPTER III

AN AGONY OF SUSPENSE

WHEN Lindbergh disappeared into the mist, an agony of suspense seized the hearts of the people on both sides of the Atlantic.

Any little quirk or catch in his 200-horsepower whirlwind Wright motor might bring instant disaster and death. The tremendous load that was to be hurled through space by that engine was greater than had ever been lifted by a motor of such power. Every airman on two continents knew the danger. Every newspaper reader, harking back to descriptions of fliers hurled to death by sudden unforeseen mishaps to their planes, waited anxiously for reports of Lindbergh's progress.

The weather had cleared all along the Atlantic coast. A wind blowing steadily from the west had swept before it the clouds that only a few hours before had menaced Lindbergh's flight. It was as though a great, loving mother with a celestial broom were sweeping from the path of a well-loved son all possible danger.

FOLLOWING THE GREAT CIRCLE

The course he had mapped for himself was the same as that which had been planned for the ill-fated flight of Nungesser and Coli, except that the course laid out by the Frenchmen was the reverse. It ran from Roosevelt Field to the Massachusetts coast and thence along

the Atlantic seaboard northward to the tip of Newfoundland.   There it ventured boldly into the open
sea, following the great circle to the coast of Ireland.
After that it was a short run with well-marked land-
falls to Paris.

The first news came from East Greenwich, Rhode
Island.   There women on their way to market heard
above them the low regular hum of a motor and caught
a swift glimpse of a gray shape in a distant cloud.   That
was 9.05 Daylight-saving time.   Thirty-five minutes
later two other women in Halifax, Massachusetts, saw
the *Spirit of St. Louis* flying so low that they could
see beneath the gray wings the capital NX211 which
identified him.

Lindbergh was now off the coast of his native America
and was speeding northward to Canada.   At 12.25 noon
fishermen near Meteghan, Nova Scotia, sighted him.
He had made his first water jump of two hundred miles
safely and his plane, relieved of part of its heavy load
of gasoline, was flying easier.   Skilfully and carefully
he had choked back his engine from the first full-
throttled blast that had been necessary to bring him
into the air.   Everything was now up to the motor and
his own determination to stay awake.   Steadily and
surely he had handled the controls, leveling off the
plane for its next leg to the tip of Newfoundland.

THE FALSE FORECAST

It was good flying weather, and if the predictions of
the weather bureau held good, he was sitting pretty.
That forecast told of continuing fair weather from
Newfoundland eastward across the Atlantic.

Photo Pacific and Atlantic Photos

HOW LINDBERGH NAVIGATED THE "SPIRIT OF ST. LOUIS"

The upper picture shows Lindbergh looking out the window of the plane, while in the lower picture is the instrument board showing the various gauges, switches and the compass which he used on the flight.

IN THE SHADOW OF THE "SPIRIT OF ST. LOUIS"

Captain Lindbergh, the owner of the great wings which carried him across the Atlantic

How false that forecast was Lindbergh was soon to learn. The impossibility of making any kind of reliable prediction about winds and weather originating in the Atlantic without offshore weather stations of some kind was afterwards to be part of his bitter comment.

He flew low over Nova Scotia and hundreds of persons marked the beautiful, gray bird. Springfield reported him at 1.05, Milford at 1.50, and Mulgrave on the Strait of Canso at 3.05.

Here at Canso Strait he saw with grave concern the first intimation of the terrible ordeal that was soon to face him. Great banks of thick fog were rolling steadily in from the Atlantic, the thermometer dropping steadily. Little needles of ice from time to time appeared on the fuselage.

Another stretch of water 200 miles long was passed and he was over Newfoundland. The fog was coming in thicker than ever and he flew low to keep out of it. At Cape Race, Newfoundland, a brisk wind was tearing the fog into mist and piling it into huge mountains.

INTO THE THICK OF THE FOG

Dusk was coming down when Lindbergh flew over St. Johns, Newfoundland, and reached the last tip of land on the American continent Carefully he circled the bare cliffs that jutted out into the Atlantic. He wanted to make sure that this was really his jumping-off place. The Great Circle, over which his earth-inductor compass was to guide him, was beneath him. It was 7.15, just eleven hours and twenty-three minutes after his start at Roosevelt Field, when he headed into the thick of the fog. The good flying weather over the

Atlantic that had been promised by the United States
Weather Bureau and the Canadian Weather Bureau
was a myth. Instead, there was the most dangerous
kind of flying weather, thick clouds more than a mile
deep pressing almost to the surface of the ocean, freezing cold that threatened every minute to develop into
a sleet storm.

It was well for Lindbergh that he was flying in a
snug, inclosed cabin. Well it was for him that his fur-
lined flying suit fitted smoothly, shutting out the chill
that seeped through every cranny of the plane. His
helmet was now pulled tight upon his young head as
he and the *St. Louis* fought to shake off the clutching
fingers of the white death that rode in that freezing
cloud bank.

THE TALONS OF THE WHITE DEATH

And then the long talons of the white death gripped
the plane in earnest. A sleet storm, deadliest of all the
dangers in aviation, raged about the *Spirit of St. Louis*.
Lindbergh knew what that meant. A plane in flight is
kept aloft by the curvature of its wings. Once let these
surfaces be flattened by such a weight as sleet, the plane
would fall like a bird shot through the heart.

It was the supreme test now of Lindbergh's skill and
courage. For an instant, and an instant only, he
debated. There was time to turn back and make a
safe landing at St. Johns. He could come down
slowly and surely in the shallow water near the shore,
using his pneumatic raft to keep him afloat. That
way lay life and another chance. The old adage, "He
who fights and runs away, may live to fight another

day" ran through his brain. He looked ahead into the impenetrable fog. The sleet was coming thicker than ever. Then he made up his mind. He would not go back. He would fight it out as he had commenced.

Like an eagle shot from some high cliff, he turned his gray wings downward until the *Spirit of St. Louis* emerged beneath the cloud bank scarcely two hundred feet from the cold, blue-green waves beneath him. Again he leveled off his ship, studied his earth-inductor compass, and sped eastward. It was bitterly cold down there, with the fog bank like a solid, gray, granite mill-stone facing downward, and the chill of the ocean like a great nether millstone beneath him.

And now fate and death pressed closer. Slowly and steadily the fog bank pressed downward, driving him lower and lower. Each time it touched the gray wings it left its heavy sleet upon the up-swelling curve.

TRAPPED LIKE A WILD THING

Lindbergh looked ahead and saw a fearful thing. A few miles before him directly in his path the upper millstone of gray touched the nether millstone of the Atlantic. He was trapped as surely as ever a wild thing had been trapped in a deadfall.

But he was not beaten yet. The spirit that had flown alone across the American continent in two great hops, and that had ventured upon this most daring of voyages across the ocean, was not through. There was still a chance. He had flown beneath the fog bank to excape the sleet. Now he must try to reach the clear air above it before the weight of sleet should force him down to defeat and perhaps to death.

Upon the instant that his resolution was made, he put it into action. The *Spirit of St. Louis*, fortunately lightened by the loss of its many gallons of spent gasoline, was angled sharply upward. Up and up they zoomed, they two, the great gray bird and the boy's soul within it. The sleet storm was round about them as they roared steeply upward. Was this the fate that had overtaken Nungesser and Coli? Was this great, cold demon to beat him down to death beneath the waves?

The needle of his altimeter showed that he was soaring at a height of more than 5000 feet above the sea level. A mile higher and still the fog and the sleet storm round about him; 8000 feet and still the fog and sleet. The gray wings were now one broad glare of ice, but shafts of pale light were coming through the fog. At 10,000 feet and through the top layer of the gray death they tore, Lindbergh and his plane, triumphant at last. It had been a climb of two miles with the bony hands of death tugging at them both every inch of the way. But now the fog lay beneath them in gently tossing hillocks of gray moisture.

Once clear of the fog, he set himself to follow the invisible line over the Great Circle by what is termed "straight-line" flying.

This does not mean that he attempted to fly the whole distance in a straight line. He attempted simply to fly in a straight line every hundred miles. At each hundred-mile point, charts showed him the exact direction in which his plane should be headed. Thus every hour, assuming that he flew one hundred miles an hour, he merely checked and changed his direction.

With the menace of the fog removed, *The Spirit of St. Louis*, lonely as a bird over all that wilderness of water, roared cheerily on its way.

NIGHT ON THE OCEAN

It was black night by this time, an inky darkness unrelieved by moonlight. There was the brightness of the great stars, of course, but they were only pinpoints in a wide-flung canopy of black velvet. Within the little cabin Lindbergh yawned sleepily. Now that the tension of the sleet storm had passed, fatigue was taking its toll. He had slept less than three hours before jumping off and the human brain was demanding the rest that was its right. Ahead of him was another fight, a fight against sleep, which might mean death.

CHAPTER IV

A Lonely Soul's Terrific Test

BENEATH the Lone Eagle the clouds of trouble lay two miles thick. For more than one thousand miles they extended directly over his course. Had he known of that terrific test of human nerve and motor reliability he would not have started. This he declared after he reached Paris. He was no flying fool to rush helter-skelter into dangers which a few days of fair weather might dissipate.

He reached into the package of sandwiches at his feet, drew forth the layers of bread and ham comprising the topmost, unwrapped the oiled paper preserving it from the fog moisture, and ate. It was instinctive, that curious, lonesome meal two miles above the ocean. Every little while the sandy-haired young man who was eating leaned toward the right to take a deep draught of water from one of the two canteens that swung beside him.

He never could tell later what was the taste of the one and one-half sandwiches he consumed nor remember the feel of the cool water within his tight-lipped mouth. His tense, athletic, fit, young body put in its automatic demand for food and drink, and like an automaton, his brain commanded his hands to supply that demand.

As a dial before him recorded each hundred miles of his journey he corrected the reading of the marvelous

(34)

earth-inductor compass by which he navigated.   These hundred-mile sections of his progress that fateful Friday night served to keep him awake.   They were more absorbing to him than any mystery story could be.   They told of lessening load in the gasoline tanks, of approaching victory.   They kept him busy through the watches of the short night.

CUTTING THE NIGHT IN HALF

For it was a short night, the briefest ever experienced by any man in that latitude.   He was flying directly toward the sun at a time when daylight lasted until nine o'clock in the evening and dawn came about four in the morning.   His speed of a little more than one hundred miles an hour cut about one hundred thirty minutes from the hours of darkness so that instead of something more than six hours of night he had something less than four hours.

It was not all blackness, for a mist-flecked moon flooded for awhile the upper surface of the fog bank with a glory of golden light shortly after he had zoomed above the clouds.   That radiance exhilarated him and seemed a beacon of hope.   He saw the masts of a ship early in the night, and later blurs of light that might have been ships.

As the fog bank lowered he sent the *Spirit of St. Louis* downward with it.   The clouds thinned and he slipped through them again until he was flying about one hundred feet above the ocean.   For mile after mile he held that level until a hailstorm made it advisable that he again seek the safety of high altitude.   For several hours after that he flew through a dense fog absolutely blind.

Lindbergh vainly tried to pierce the enveloping fog. He flew high, and still above him was the dense, gray mist.   He dropped in a succession of careful dives until he had almost reached the surface of the ocean, and still the fog closed him in.   There was nothing for it but to go straight on shutting out with the bolts of iron nerves the fears that would have overwhelmed any other man.

THE SUPREME TEST

Now was the supreme test applied to the lonely soul of Lindbergh and the motor that was the soul of his plane.   A momentary shaking of the man's high courage, an instant of panic would undo all that had been so bravely done.   Any one of a hundred little mishaps in the smoothly purring motor, and death would triumph over the daring combination of man and his machine.

There was a flaw, a mishap that would have brought disaster had it been placed elsewhere.   A crack in a fuel tank of the *Spirit of St. Louis* appeared.   Fortunately it was near the top of the tank and the precious gasoline had sunk below it before it came.   Lindbergh was to learn of it later as the result of a French mechanic's vigilant search.

A steady fate like a beacon led him on.   He knew the dawn was not far away.   His calculations showed that the short night would soon pass, and with it he believed the fog would lift. Again and again the cool trickle of fresh water from the canteen beside

THE OFFICIAL GREETING OF FRANCE

The "Lone Eagle" with President Doumergue of France and Ambassador Herrick. Lindbergh is wearing the Cross of the Legion of Honor, just presented to him by President Doumergue.

LINDBERGH'S FIRST CALL IN FRANCE

The American flier's visit of sympathy to Madame Nungesser, mother of France's intrepid war ace, who, with his companion, Coli, was missing after an attempt to fly from Paris to New York.

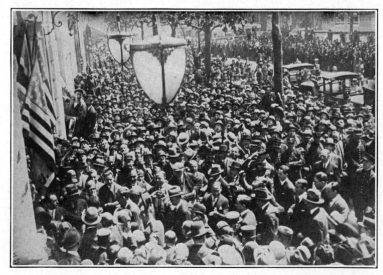

THE PARIS CROWDS WILD WITH ENTHUSIASM

A few of the people in the French capital anxious to catch a glimpse of Lindbergh.

him quenched his thirst and soothed his parched throat.

DAWN ON THE OCEAN

Never was dawn more heartening to a human being than that which came, gray and chill. As the light increased the mists lifted from the face of the sea and the Lone Eagle saw through the periscope of his blind plane feathery clouds ahead that told of clearing weather. He noted beside him white gulls flying tirelessly, easily, in the same direction he was going. He saw them drift effortlessly to the calm bosom of the sea and thence rise serenely to resume their journey.

"There," he said, later speaking of his impressions of that dawn, "is true flight, a marvelous conquest of both wind and wave."

Now the agony of suspense was almost over for him. The fog had shredded away into nothingness and a fair May morning smiled from every dancing wave. His abnormal eyes, their vision double that of the average man, searched the onrushing horizon.

"Come, you Ireland!" was his constant thought. He had burned into his brain the topography of this land from which one of his ancestors had come. "Ireland," he said, "is green and mountainous. I will be sure to know it."

THE MIRAGE—AND IRELAND

And then as noon drew near, a strange thing happened. Before him out of the waves slowly appeared a shore line, at first low and gray, then. as it assumed form, green and high. Cliffs reared their bold, purple fronts, and distant mountains raised black peaks with cloud wreaths on their brows.

He could scarcely believe what his eyes saw. Here, long before what his maps indicated, was Ireland directly in his path. Here were the green valleys and the rock-sided mountains. Closely he studied his instrument board. His well-thumbed map was again scrutinized.

Even as he looked, the mountains faded, the green valleys disappeared. It was only a fair promise, that picture that had caused his pulses to race, his brain to disbelieve his eyes. "It was a mirage," he said later, telling of the vision at a banquet. "It was exactly what I had pictured Ireland to be. It was only when the picture faded from the clouds that I realized what had happened."

And then, even as he mourned the vanished shore line, the breakers of Dingle Bay were before him. Low he flew and fast with the goal before him. Now, whatever happened, he was safe. Landmarks aplenty were beneath him. It was afternoon and the beacons of England and fair France were just ahead.

CHAPTER V

Paris—and Victory

OVER the Channel they roared happily, the *Spirit of St. Louis* and the son of the Vikings. France at last with a miraculous twilight revealing the roads over which other young Americans had poured ten years before.

That dark steeple with its flaring apex must be Eiffel Tower. Paris with its boulevards lay like a cobweb of light below him. He must get ready for a careful, feather-light landing. Would anybody be around to take care of his plane?

He felt the pocket of his tunic. Those letters of introduction. There they were, particularly the one to Ambassador Herrick. Gee! Wouldn't a bed feel good! Was that Le Bourget straight ahead? He would fly low. Lights coming on and off. Maybe it wasn't! Better buzz around to see if there were any other lighted field.

Nope! Better fly back. That must be Le Bourget, after all. Off with the throttle. Easy, girl. Flatten out! Gee, whillikens, what a crowd! Too late to flip her up again. Steady! Hey, look out for that propeller! Look at them running toward us, thousands of them, millions!

Around him they milled, the cheering, mad crowd, delirious with joy. Lindbergh was half pushed, half pulled from his cabin. For an instant he straightened, his bladelike young form towering above the throng.

"I am Charles A. Lindbergh," he said, his hand reaching for his six letters of introduction.

Then they mounted him on their shoulders and bore him from the field.

BEFORE THE ARRIVAL OF LINDBERGH

More than one hundred thousand persons were in that delirious throng. They had come to Le Bourget in an unending stream, beginning at noon. As the night advanced all roads leading to the great flying field were blocked with streams of traffic. The restaurant across the road from the hangars had been unable to supply the demand for food.

Ambassador Herrick and a receiving party composed of the most notable men of Paris awaited in a hangar. Rumors shot through the crowd like electric impulses. "He was forced down at Cherbourg."   "He had lost his way."   "He was only ten miles from Paris." "He had not yet passed over England."   The mighty throng believed or disbelieved, according to the pessimism or optimism of its units.

The flares shot their radiance skyward. The famous searchlight of Le Bourget, the world's most powerful beacon, pierced the blackness and the clouds.

Suddenly above the babble and the murmur, quick ears caught the droning of a motor. "It is he!" shouted hundreds. Those with keenest eyes saw a gray shape high in the heavens. It drifted away almost as soon as it was glimpsed. "Only a searching plane looking for Lindbergh," said some and the explanation was accepted.

But it was Lindbergh, making his first hesitating

turn over the field before seeking elsewhere the field
of his destination.   Before the excitement caused by
that dim shape in the clouds had subsided, the great
moment arrived.   Out of the north like a noiseless,
celestial visitor, a great bird appeared, silver-gray in
the rays of the beacon.   It floated toward the multitude
as all eyes were drawn toward it and all breathing
seemed to cease.   It was Lindbergh coming down upon
the field with a "dead stick."   Skilfully and with
infinite care to avoid injuring any of the throng about
him, he made a feather-light landing as a roar, "Vive
Lindbergh!" went up from one hundred thousand
throats and the mass of humanity dashed over him
like a wave.

RESCUED FROM THE CROWD

It was a herculean feat to rescue the Eagle from the
mass that wanted to touch him with one hundred thousand pairs of hands.   "Save my ship!" he cried as he
was borne along on the crest of the wave.   An excited
Parisian brandishing a cane to clear a path, struck
Lindbergh a whack on the head that raised a lump.
His flying helmet that he had started to carry was
torn from his clasp and disappeared forever.   Ruthless
souvenir hunters' sharp knives hacked away square
pieces of the plane's gray canvas sides.

Lindbergh never knew how he reached the side of
the Ambassador, nor how they were taken to a smaller
building in which the lights were promptly extinguished
so that the crowd might not find them.   Together he
and the Ambassador stumbled over fields and down
a dark road to the Ambassador's waiting motor.   After

an hour's battle with tides of traffic they came to Paris by a roundabout route and Lindbergh once more was upon American soil in the Embassy of his native land.

He was too excited and too tired to sleep. A little soup and several glasses of milk were his only food requirements. The Ambassador fitted him out with an Ambassadorial bathrobe, and a warm bath was turned on for him.

It was now about three o'clock and the newspaper men had finally located him. With them he chatted for a quarter of an hour until the Ambassador smilingly commanded him to go to bed. Outside, all Paris seemed to be wide awake and talking of the tired young man's achievement. He looked out of the windows on the lights of the beautiful city. His tall, young frame stiffened with a mighty stretch and a jaw-cracking yawn; he laid aside the Ambassadorial bathrobe, switched off the electric light, letting his tired body feel briefly the luxury of cool linen, and dropped dreamlessly into a deep well of sleep.

CHAPTER VI

An American Breakfast

THE little gold clock in the reception room of the American Embassy tinkled one stroke when the news that Lindbergh had awakened sped through the quiet house. Ten hours had passed since sleep had come to Lindbergh and the Embassy was besieged by a crowd of photographers with still and moving cameras, reporters, and thousands of Parisians clamoring for a glimpse of the hero. At twelve o'clock noon the Ambassador had opened quietly Lindbergh's bedroom door. The young flier had sighed softly and turned in his sleep. Now the water in the tub was splashing gaily and the orders for silence were off for the day.

The Ambassador, bred in Ohio and knowing what a healthy young American preferred for breakfast, had ransacked the markets of Paris for that first French meal of Lindbergh. It was exactly what the flier would have ordered in an American hotel. Here waiting was a grapefruit, perfectly chilled, oatmeal with real cream, bacon and eggs, crisp buttered toast, and real coffee.

At his bedside was a double-breasted suit of blue serge. Parmalee Herrick, the Ambassador's son, had requisitioned it from one of the house servants. Lindbergh's khaki suit obviously was not the thing for the Parisian boulevards. All efforts to match in size

Lindbergh's big tan army shoes had been a failure. These, however, had been brushed until they shone. The suit fit, as Lindbergh expressed it, "too quick" across the shoulders, and the sleeves and the trouser legs were a little short, but he accepted it with the same glad, gay mood that he accepted everything.

HIS OWN STORY OF THE FLIGHT

The waiting crowd in front of the Embassy by this time knew that he was awake and was shouting for him. With the Ambassador at his side he went to a window and gave a sample of the smile that Paris was to love. Then the newspaper men claimed him as their own and he told in direct, brief fashion, the fashion of a clear-thinking young American, his first story of the flight.

"Being newspapermen," he began, "I suppose you gentlemen are interested first in knowing what was the most dangerous thing about our flight. The most dangerous thing of all was that landing at Le Bourget, bringing that ship down on a field with all that crowd running. I had more fear at that moment for the welfare of our plane than at any other time in the whole flight.

"The first part of the flight was better and easier than any of us expected. The field in New York was muddy, which made the take-off a little long, but we got away all right.

"All the way up the American coast to Newfoundland we had uncommonly good weather—lots better than we expected. But for the next 1000 miles it couldn't have been much worse for us."

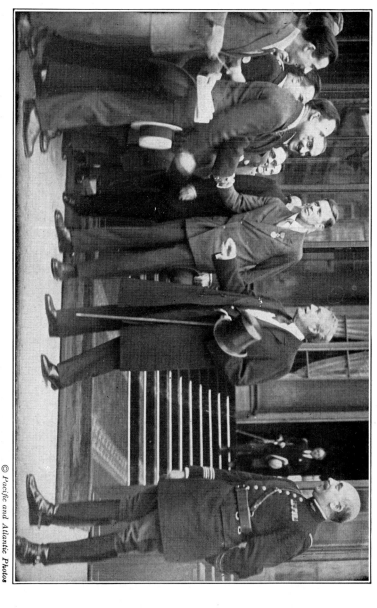

FRANCE'S GREAT MEN GATHER TO HONOR LINDBERGH

The "Lone Eagle" receiving the congratulations of the distinguished citizens of France. On his left is Ambassador Herrick and on his lapel is the cross of the Legion of Honor.

SALUTING THE COLORS

Captain Lindbergh with Ambassador Herrick greets the standard
of the 34th Regiment of Aviation of France.

HURRAY FOR LINDY!

Ambassador Herrick leads the cheering on the steps of the
American Embassy in Paris.

At this juncture Ambassador Herrick remarked, "When Lindbergh says 'we' he means the ship and himself."

All the way through, except when asked for a personal opinion of something, the flier used the first person plural in describing the voyage.

"After we got away from land," continued the aviator, "we ran into fog, then into rain, then hail. Sometimes we flew not more than ten feet above the water, and the highest was 10,000 feet. We went up that high to try to get above the storm, but the average altitude for the whole second 1000 miles of the flight was less than 100 feet.

"If we had known that the weather would be as bad over that part of the ocean as it turned out to be, we would not have started, but once we got into it there wasn't any use in turning back; there wasn't anything to do but keep going.

"We were mighty happy to see the dawn, which we ran into about two o'clock, New York time.

"In the afternoon we picked up Ireland. From the maps we had and from what I read home I knew that England was a sort of hilly, rolling country, France pretty flat, and Ireland inclined to be mountainous. So when I saw pretty high ridges off in front I knew it was Ireland. I—"

SIR ALAN COBHAM ASKS A FEW QUESTIONS

"Pardon me"—a voice from the outer ring of listeners called—"but did you do the whole flight by dead reckoning? I am a flier myself; my name is Cobham, and I flew over here from London a few minutes ago to see you and tell you that you have done the greatest thing I have ever heard of."

All heads turned. The voice was that of Sir Alan Cobham, the greatest of British long-distance aviators, the pioneer of routes to South Africa, India, and Australia.

"It is Sir Alan Cobham," several said, and made a path for him to approach Lindbergh, who grasped the Briton's hand and said: "I am mighty glad to meet you, sir. I have heard a great deal about you."

"What I want to know most," said the Englishman, "is, did you steer by dead reckoning?"

"I had to," replied Lindbergh. "There were no hands for a sextant. I used an earth-inducting compass called a pioneer earth inductor, and it brought me to the coast of Ireland within three miles of the Great Circle indications.

"Steered by dead reckoning from Cherbourg to Paris, too, and hit Paris. It was the compass that did it."

"What about gasoline?" asked Cobham.

"About 448 gallons when I started and only burned twelve gallons an hour (which would have made 402 gallons), so I could have flown another 1000 miles."

HOW LINDBERGH KEPT AWAKE

"How did you keep awake?" Cobham wanted to know.

"I didn't get sleepy," said Lindbergh. "You see, I did not have the wind in my face, being down in the cockpit, and that is the secret of that."

He then told Cobham his total food for the trip was

a sandwich and a half and one cup of water. Asked if the flight made him believe commercial transatlantic flights were feasible, he said:

"Yes, if there were landing places; big mid-ocean landing fields. It is too big a jump without them."

"You think it will come in five years?" he was asked.

"Oh, sooner than that," he replied.

Someone asked if he was going to fly back.

"I don't see any real reason to," he said.

"What points did you fly over in crossing from Ireland to France?" someone asked.

"Hand me the map; I'll tell you," Lindbergh replied.

"How did you fly from Cherbourg on to Paris?"

"Oh, just came on in a straight line, picked up the beams of the searchlights all right and saw the Seine. Then when I got a look at Eiffel Tower all lit up, I knew that was Paris, and I had been told at home that Le Bourget was fourteen kilometers northeast of Paris.

"When I got there I wasn't quite sure that it was Le Bourget. That is why I flew around there several minutes. I thought Le Bourget must be a little further on, but when they turned on the field lights I figured that must be the place. Then the crowd began racing out there into the lights, and there wasn't any more doubt about it."

THE FATE OF NUNGESSER AND COLI

The French journalists asked Lindbergh what was his opinion as to the fate of Nungesser and Coli, as he took a path through much the same route they were expected to follow.

"There are a hundred things that could have happened to Nungesser and Coli," he said. "If they had very bad weather this side of Newfoundland, one of the hundred things that seems not improbable is that they got into a sleet storm that they might not have been able to get out of or climb above. A sleet storm can bring you down in five minutes, because ice built up in front of the wings will change their entire curve.

"Then suppose they flew low all the way and got into an ice field. There you have got the worst possible conditions, and you might not be able to get over it. There are ice fields off Newfoundland where, if you had to come down, there wouldn't be one chance in a thousand to be found.

"The flight Nungesser and Coli took from Paris to New York is much harder than coming from New York to Paris because of unfavorable conditions. At New York we received telegrams from all over the United States, nearly all asking us to express sorrow to the people of Paris over the loss of Nungesser and Coli. Their attempt touched the heart of everybody in our country, and every one of us wanted them to succeed."

CHAPTER VII

Lindbergh, the Dutiful Son

SCARCELY had the hero of the air finished his chat with the correspondents and submitted to the wishes of the photographers when his thoughts flew to his mother. It was not enough that he should cable to her and she to him. He wanted to hear her voice.

"I'd like to hop over to London and talk to my mother on the new transatlantic phone," he said.

"You won't have to go to London," said the Ambassador with a smile. "We thought of all that and a special hookup has been arranged."

A PHONE CALL 4300 MILES AWAY

For hours work had been rushed upon the hookup for the telephone call the Ambassador had foreseen would be wanted by his youthful charge. Now all was ready and the call was put through from the Embassy to the modest little home in Detroit where a mother sat anxiously waiting. The line was finally cleared, a Detroit operator said, "Paris is ready," and the voice of Charles A. Lindbergh came under and over 4300 miles of land and sea to his mother's ear.

"Hello, mother," he called.

"Hello, son," she replied.

"The trip over was wonderful," he went on.

"How are you feeling?" she cut in. "Are you very tired?"

"No, I am feeling fine. Don't worry about me. Everybody is wonderful to me."

Again the mother's voice interrupted, "Take care of yourself, Charles. Get plenty of rest. You have passed through a tremendous strain. Be careful or you will break down."

The eager young voice in Paris was vibrant. "Oh, I'm all right. I have had ten hours' sleep and a fine breakfast. I am going out for an automobile ride after a while."

And there were words of love too sacred and intimate for repetition. Every mother and every loving son may reconstruct that talk to his fancy. There was a click as the connection was broken and two persons 4300 miles apart turned shining faces to the world.

AT THE HOME OF MADAME NUNGESSER

It was fitting that Lindbergh should go from that talk with his mother to the home of the mother of Nungesser, the missing airman of France. With him went Ambassador Herrick, while motor cycles cleared the path for them through the crowded streets. Outside the unpretentious Nungesser home, the crowd assembled magically.

The Ambassador introduced Lindbergh to Mme. Nungesser and she instantly clasped him to her bosom as her tears flowed unrestrainedly. They met in the same dining room where mother and son ate their last meal before their parting. It was some moments before Lindbergh collected himself sufficiently to speak.

"I wanted to make my first call on the mother of my valiant friend, Captain Nungesser," he said haltingly. "I knew Charles in New York and admired his spirit. I have high hope that he will be found. I want you to have confidence that he will be found. My own mother was confident that I would be safe at the end of my journey."

Carefully the Ambassador translated each sentence as Mme. Nungesser nodded to show that she understood.

"With the whole American people I regret that the searches made for Charles and his companion, the brave Coli, up to now," continued Lindbergh, "have been unfruitful, but I want you to keep on hoping."

The brave mother looked at him as she placed both hands upon his shoulders.

"I am a mother, that is all," she said. "I have not lost hope of seeing my son again. The heart of a French woman knows how to support suffering and anxiety."

And now her voice broke into heart-tearing sobs. She told how sorry she was she could not have been at Le Bourget to see him descend in triumph. As the Ambassador translated her broken sentences, Lindbergh patted her gently on the shoulder and told her of his own mother and their love for each other. Still weeping, she went with him to the door and as he passed over the threshold, embraced him in farewell.

GREETED BY THE NOTABLES AT THE EMBASSY

As he passed into the streets, he noted that American flags were everywhere and that Old Glory flew above

the Quai d'Orsay for the first time since President
Wilson arrived in Paris.   Back at the Embassy a
procession of notables greeted him.   Paul Claudel,
French Ambassador to the United States, Jean Borotra,
the famous tennis player, M. Scapini, president of the
Association of Veterans Blinded in the War, Marshal
Lyautey, and a messenger from the Foreign Office
bearing the felicitations of Foreign Minister Aristide
Briand, were in the long line.   Messages from King
Alfonso of Spain, Premier Mussolini of Italy, Sir
Samuel Hoare, British Air Minister, King Gustav of
Sweden, and a host of others were piled high on the
Embassy table.   Flowers filled two rooms and the
telephone called insistently and continuously.

Ambassador Herrick took him for an eye-filling drive
in the city, where thousands stopped to cheer the face
now everyone knew.   In the evening a little dinner
party in the Embassy brought the happy day to a
close and Lindbergh went to bed knowing he must be
up and about early to meet the most formidable round
of receptions that any man of recent years had faced.

CHAPTER VIII

A Knight in Borrowed Clothes

LINDBERGH awoke on Monday morning from another night of heavy, dreamless sleep to find a tailor and his assistants, a shoe dealer with a huge pile of shoe boxes, and a haberdasher with shirts, ties, underwear, socks, and collars, waiting for him.

The tailors performed their rites, and the selection of haberdashery was only a matter of a few minutes. The shoes presented a tougher problem. The young flier, like most American country boys of his inches, has extraordinarily big feet. It was not until twelve pairs of the largest sizes in the shoe dealer's stock had been tried that one perfectly fitting pair was found.

He was still arrayed in the blue, double-breasted suit of borrowed clothes when he went to breakfast, the same American breakfast to provide which Ambassador Herrick had ransacked the markets the day before. The street in front of the Embassy was crowded when he emerged to motor with the Ambassador to Le Bourget. His ship had been his most dominant thought during the past twenty-four hours. He was fearful that some damage had been done by the crowd, and he wanted to test everything with his own sensitive hands and keenest of eyes.

All the way to Le Bourget the crowds recognized and cheered him. Arriving at the hangar, where he was greeted warmly by French fliers, he was told that nothing serious had happened to the *Spirit of St. Louis*. He was shown a tiny crack in the top of a gasoline tank, a defect which if it had gone lower might have had serious consequences. He smiled as the holes in the fuselage were pointed out to him. These were caused by the souvenir hounds who had cut out squares of canvas on the night of the arrival. The proposition of a French company to put the plane in perfect condition was accepted by him. The inspection of the planes in the hangars that lined the field, and chats with French aviators filled the rest of a morning, which to him was absorbingly interesting. Luncheon in the Embassy was a respite, during which Ambassador Herrick rehearsed with him the ceremonies that were to come.

It was early afternoon when, with the Ambassador, he motored to the Élysée Palace to receive from President Doumergue the Cross of the Legion of Honor. This came in the course of a ceremony as brief as it was impressive. The President of France gave to him the congratulations of the French nation, told of the unfailing friendship between France and America and pinned upon the borrowed coat of the Knight of the Air the famous Cross of the Legion of Honor. And then, as Lindbergh blushed to the roots of his sandy hair, the President stood on tiptoes and kissed him on both cheeks.

The appearance of the American youth before and after the ceremony was in sharp contrast to that of the group around him. His badly fitting blue suit and borrowed brown felt hat set him apart from the shining silk hats, black, long-tailed coats, and gray and black striped trousers of the diplomats.

As he turned to go away, President Doumergue called him back.

"I want you to take this message to your mother," he said in French. "Tell her for me that she has a wonderful son. He has won the admiration of the French people for his splendid courage and his unique achievement."

Ambassador Herrick translated, and Lindbergh blushed again as the diplomats applauded.

Photographers in the courtyard of the palace made shots of Lindbergh wearing his decorations, as a broad grin split the face of the flier.

The rest of the afternoon was given over to a reception tendered by the Aëro Club of France. The assembly hall was thronged to the doors when Lindbergh arose and said:

"Friends, I am not going to attempt to express the gratitude which I feel at the wonderful reception you have given me. That is beyond expression. I merely wish to convey a message from the American people to our comrades, the people of France.

"We in the United States realize that the heroic effort of our brothers of the French soil, Nungesser and Coli, was a far greater project than the one completed Saturday night. They knew they were heading into terrible weather conditions and were beset by almost inconceivable dangers. My people have felt the loss of Nungesser and Coli almost as much as you have. Their grief is surpassed only by your own. But they have not given up hope back there in America that the brave French airmen may yet be found somewhere in the wilds of Newfoundland or Canada."

Ambassador Herrick was cheered wildly when he said: "Who can say, after seeing this boy here land his little plane almost on the same spot where Nungesser and Coli took off—who can say after seeing the great welcome that the people of France are giving this young son of Uncle Sam—that the magnificent friendship that has existed for 150 years between America and France is not an internal, indestructible and genuine feeling? I want you to know, my dear friends of France, that this young Lochinvar from the West brings to you the spirit of the American Republic—the spirit not only of the youth of the land, but of old age as well."

Minister of War Painleve reviewed the history of aviation and hailed Lindbergh as a true interpreter between the spirits of France and the United States. Paul Claudel, French Ambassador to the United States, brought an emotional climax when he proposed a toast to *La mère courageuse*, the mother of Lindbergh.

Another honor came to the flier when, after the Aëro Club reception, he motored with Ambassador Herrick to the Ministry of Finance, where he met Minister Raymond Poincaré. "You have accomplished the impossible," he told Lindbergh. "This feat of yours will bring together France and the United States as nothing else could have done."

An informal dinner in the Embassy brought the day to a close. After it Lindbergh had one of his characteristically informal chats with the newspaper men. It was almost impossible to get him to express opinions upon anything other than aviation. A light note came when he was asked what he thought of Paris.

"It's fine," he said. "I cannot tell too much how I like it. I would like to see a lot more of it, particularly at night."

There was a roar of laughter as one of the newspaper men suggested a trip to Montmartre.   Lindbergh's face was serious as he suggested that he did not mean exactly that, but that he would like to see the beauty of the lighted boulevards.

"Are you going up in the Eiffel Tower?" he was asked.

"I do not know," he replied.   "I flew around it the night I arrived and saw it from the outside.   Maybe I will go up to see what it looks like."   A number of like questions, some of them foolish, were neatly turned off with some such answer as "I have no opinion about that," and "That's another of the same kind."

His reserve dropped over him like a cloak when the talk was about his mother.   Someone inquired if she had not intended to fly with him over the Atlantic. "No," he replied.   "We never even thought about that, although she has flown with me a number of times when I carried mail."

He explained the intricacies of the earth-inductor compass with the precision of a scientific professor.

"We would not probably have got far off the line with just an ordinary compass," he said, "but with the earth-inductor compass you don't get such wide variations off the true north in different points of the globe.   It is more accurate and less fatiguing.   The fact that we came on to the Irish coast just three miles away from where I had expected to was merely a coincidence.   On the other hand, if we had been 100 miles away, it would not have been a coincidence.   There would not have been any danger of missing land even with an ordinary compass, because your maximum variation of error would not amount to more than 200 miles."

At odd moments during the day he was visited by some of the most famous personages in France. He beamed with pleasure when General Pershing came to congratulate him, and again when Paul Claudel, the poet ambassador, embraced him and told him of his joy. The desk in his suite was piled high with messages from every civilized country. These he read until drowsiness overtook him.

CHAPTER IX

Feted by His Home Folks

FIVE thousand excited Americans strove for the six hundred places at the American Club luncheon which was given at the Hotel Ambassador in Captain Lindbergh's honor on Tuesday. Those who were unfortunate in not being able to squeeze into the comparatively small dining room stood outside the building and shouted themselves hoarse until the boy appeared.

Paris took advantage of the long luncheon period, which is its daily hour of relaxation, to pack the boulevards and streets for a glimpse of the American hero. A narrow passageway to the hotel was maintained by the resplendent municipal guards, in their black and gold uniforms; but it took fifteen minutes for the stalwart members of the Reception Committee to force a way, with their guest, through the enthusiastic throng. Throughout the tumult of acclaim, the transcontinental flier maintained a smiling, calm face, and bowed boyishly right and left.

At the table of honor were grouped most of the prominent Americans in Paris, and many distinguished Frenchmen. Among the latter were Henry Bataille, Andre Citroen, the automobile king of France, the Comte de Castelane, Vice President of the Municipal Council of Paris.

Autographing scores of papers kept the young flier

busy for an hour. A guard was finally placed about the table to enable him to partake of the food. No sooner had he started, than word was taken to Ambassador Herrick that 200 masons and carpenters in a large building opposite the hotel had ceased work and told their foreman they would not proceed again until they had had a glimpse of Lindbergh. When the airman was told of this he said, "Oh, let me go out on the balcony for a minute."

The guests, who knew nothing of the circumstances, wondered why Lindbergh, who started across the room, was leaving so soon. When he reached the balcony he looked down upon a sea of 25,000 faces. A great shout went up; hats were thrown recklessly into the air; and whistles blew from the steam cranes. Together, Ambassador Herrick and Lindbergh waved American and French flags as the crowd continued its roaring. Traffic was stopped, and every man, woman, and child in Paris, it seemed, was jammed into the street. With a final wave of the flags, and a long, boyish smile, Lindbergh left the balcony and hurried back to the choice food which had been prepared for him.

With extraordinary insight, Percy Peixotto, president of the American Club, realizing every man in the room was eager to hear Lindbergh speak, introduced him with the brief words, "Fellow citizens, Captain Charles A. Lindbergh."

A burst of applause greeted the boy as he rose to his feet. When the deafening roar had subsided he said:

"Gentlemen, I am not going to try to express my appreciation for my reception in France, for I would not be able to do so in words.   I believe, however, it would be more interesting for me to tell you something about my flight from New York.   Public speaking is not my business, but before I go on allow me to express my great appreciation of this banquet.

"We first thought of this flight last fall in St. Louis after a very successful aëronautical meeting.   We decided to keep St. Louis and aëronautics in the foreground, and a Paris flight seemed the greatest achievement toward this goal.

"It meant more to us than anything else, as France was the ultimate end of the trip, for we decided then that after leaving America there was no other country we would rather land in after leaving the United States than France."

This was the occasion for another wild outburst, and when it quieted down Lindbergh, whose oratorical abilities, as well as clever diplomacy, have surprised everyone, continued:

"The name of my ship, the *Spirit of St. Louis,* is intended to convey a certain meaning to the people of France, and I sincerely hope it has.

"We considered the tri-motor idea for the trip, but finally chose a single motor, because it has greater cruising range.   One pilot was decided upon, because 300 gallons more fuel could be taken aboard and because with the long distance to be covered this additional fuel might have easily been the difference between failure and success.

"The Wright whirlwind motor is, I think, the best in the United States.

"After four days' test in San Diego, during which

time Nungesser and Coli left on their courageous trip, we struck off for St. Louis, arriving there in 14 hours 7 minutes.   After a few hours at St. Louis we went on to New York in 7 hours 15 minutes.

"The motor has been sixty-one hours in the air, constantly in motion, and there is no apparent difficulties or depreciation of any kind.

"This fact alone demonstrates the reliability of the commercial motors today and the trip itself the practicability of transatlantic flying under certain fixed conditions.

"I took off suddenly when I did because it seemed to be the best opportunity."

Following a detailed description of the flight, Captain Lindbergh concluded as follows:

"Well, gentlemen, the time is getting short now and I don't believe I can say any more here.   I hope I have not taken up too much of your time.   I will quit now."

Shouts and applause again reverberated through the room, as, with a little bow, the American hero sat down.

A TRIBUTE TO THE HEROIC MOTHER

Thanking Lindbergh for the honor of his presence, Mr. Peixotto paid a tribute to the flier's mother:

"To that heroic woman, his mother, we, the Americans of Paris, send our respectful homage.   Three cheers for Lindbergh, pioneer of a new era."

Ambassador Herrick was the next speaker.

"You notice," he said, "that he always says 'we,' and maybe some of you gentlemen are perplexed, but for your information I will explain he means the 'ship and I.' He is undergoing an endurance test right now equal to that of the flight and he has to hop off to other big engagements.

"All of the world loves a good sport, all of the world loves courage and bravery. We are constantly seeking for the ultimate in these things and this young Lochinvar from the West has them both. We've found him and we are happy.

"The sporting instinct, I am sorry to say, does not seem to be in politics. I suggest that all of these troubles of the world be turned over to sporting men, and being American and somewhat partial, I suggest that this bright-eyed boy act as the chairman of that committee."

Just before the speeches began, General Gouraud, the one-armed hero of the World War and one of the most loved men in France, paid tribute to the American airman. He hastened to the guest table, grasped the youth's hand and kissed him warmly on each cheek as the guests cheered loudly.

"You are a brave young man and a hero, and I wish to salute you," said the General.

Lindbergh's voice was deep with emotion as he thanked the Frenchman.

CONFIDENCE—AND PREPAREDNESS

An amusing incident, which shows, as much as anything, the confidence which the intrepid American had in his enterprise, came to light. In the pocket of his woolen shirt, with the letters of introduction which he had obtained, fearing that he would be lonesome in

Paris, since he knew no one there, was an order for his passage home on the White Star Line. The order had been issued at St. Louis, and obtained for the boy by Harry H. Knight, one of Captain Lindbergh's backers and a personal friend of many years.

From the moment of his arrival in the French capital, Lindbergh was deluged with tempting offers from various sources, all of which were promptly turned down by the American.

"This flight was not undertaken for money," he reiterated many times, "its main object was the advancement of aëronautical science."

CHAPTER X

The Highest Honors of France

THE most significant reception to Captain Lindbergh since his arrival in France came on Wednesday, when he was a guest of the members of the French Chamber of Deputies. It was not a regular session of that body, yet four-fifths of the members, who might easily have been excused, were gathered in the reception room of the President's residence, when Lindbergh and Ambassador Herrick, accompanied by the Embassy staff, arrived at three o'clock.

The applause which greeted him as he appeared continued several minutes. President Bouisson met him and extended to him a welcome from the Parliament of France. After shaking hands with the many who were closest to him, he crossed the room and listened carefully to the interpreter, while General Girod, President of the Army Commission of the Chamber, acclaimed him in the name of his colleagues and congratulated him on "the happy realization of the most audacious feat of the century."

"It is not only two continents which you have united," he said, "but the hearts of all men everywhere in admiration for that simple courage of a man which does great things. You have won the greatest of all victories, such a victory for progress as makes all men proud, such a victory as is most honorable and most worth while. Your victory is over nature, over that obstinate trio of time, space, and matter, against which man's fight must be incessant if he is to progress.

"How proud aviation is of you, her latest victor! You are of those who have said and proved that nothing is impossible. You in your youth belong to that glorious band of whom M. Bleriot, standing now beside you, was one, who have opened the great spaces.

"Magnificent hero and dear heart, we greet you in the name also of those others of your countrymen who in the Lafayette Escadrille died here for France, who like you helped to frame that unalterable fraternity, that indissoluble friendship which unites our two peoples."

Deeply moved by this tribute to his young countryman, Ambassador Herrick turned to Lindbergh, inviting him to reply. But the youth asked the Ambassador to speak first.

"I knew France," said the Ambassador, "before the war; I knew you during that dreadful ordeal, and I have known you during your magnificent restoration. Always in my heart there has been the wish that somehow I could show you more of my own country as I know it and love it. In these last days I have known the realization of that ambition.

"Gentlemen, I present to you this new Ambassador of the United States, whom France has so warmly taken to her heart."

An undercurrent of intense excitement ran over the assembled guests as Lindbergh rose to speak. The deferential shyness which had manifested itself when he was first thrown into the midst of the deputies had been displaced as he arose by a calmness and dignity that astonished men old in the ways of diplomacy. He was no longer a shy young man, but a strong, vibrant personality without self-consciousness.

"Gentlemen," he began, looking around and speaking clearly so that everyone could hear, "one hundred and thirty-two years ago Benjamin Franklin was asked, 'But what good is your balloon?   What will it accomplish?'   And he replied, 'What good is your newborn child?'"

"Less than twenty years ago, when I was not far advanced from infancy, M. Bleriot, here beside me, flew across the English Channel and he was asked, 'What good is your airplane?   What will it accomplish?'"

"Today those same skeptics might well ask me what good has been my flight from New York to Paris. My answer is that I believe it is the forerunner of a great air service from America to France, from America to Europe, which will bring our peoples together, nearer in understanding and in friendship than they have ever been."

Eloquence could never have had the effect that these simple, direct words had upon those representatives of France.

"He is a modern Parsifal, this 'Flying Fool,' " exclaimed a deputy.

"All Parsifals are fools to ordinary people," said another.

CHAPTER XI

A Triumphal Procession—One Automobile Long

THE strangest, shortest triumphal procession the world has ever known thrilled Paris on Thursday, May 26, when more than half a million Parisians thronged the streets to hail Captain Lindbergh. It was a procession one automobile long.

The French government had set aside that day to do him honor because it was "Ascension Day," a public and religious holiday. The ovation in the streets was the prelude to a superb official reception in the historic Hôtel de Ville, the city hall of Paris. Ten thousand invitations had been issued for the function and all had been accepted. Diplomats in gold lace, women in handsome gowns, men of the highest rank were in that throng. It was a day of which a Napoleon might be proud.

With Ambassador Herrick and the President of the Municipal Council, Captain Lindbergh left the Embassy at three o'clock. The car proceeded slowly down the wide Champs Élysées, which resembled a turbulent black sea rolling and bobbing up and down with the thousands of excited Parisians. Like a huge dam, policemen and the Republican Guards stood in a solid line to keep back the surging mass of humanity which threatened, as at Le Bourget Field on the night of his arrival, the safety of the young aviator.

The enthusiasm of the French had not abated through the five days of unprecedented homage to a

private citizen, which preceded the festivities. The
hundreds of thousands who saw him pass through the
streets were the same wild enthusiasts who began to
greet him when all the world knew he had conquered
the Atlantic. Men, women, and children shouted,
hats were thrown into the air, and flowers bestrewed
his path. The more emotional of the crowd reached
forward to bestow a kiss, if possible, or touch his hand.

A KING COMES TO FRANCE

The eyes of the crowds were fixed on the slight, young
figure of the American who had overcome the greatest
hazards of aëronavigation. Men who would have
gained acclaim on other occasions were passed by without recognition. Myron T. Herrick, the American
Ambassador, General Godin, the president of Municipal Council, and M. Chiappe, prefect of the police,
who accompanied the aviator, were lay figures in the
tableau, and passed unnoticed before the wet, shining
eyes of the French enthusiasts. A king had come to
them, a king with a new kind of crown, the crown of
bravery, and Paris paid homage to it such as few mon-
archs have enjoyed.

Impressive tributes had been paid to him by the
highest officials of France, before he was greeted by
the crowds in the streets. Marshal Foch and Marshal
Joffre had praised his feat at a visit to Marshal Foch's
home. Wearing the insignia of the American Distinguished Service Medal, the veteran generalissimo
said that the exploit of Lindbergh showed "what a
young man can do when he is well prepared for his
attempt and when he has the courage to see it through."

"The entire French nation is proud of your success," declared the hero of the early years of the war, Marshal Joffre.

TEMPORARY AMERICAN AMBASSADOR

Each place he visited on the long program for the day showed evidence of the affection which the French had for this simple youth. "The Temporary American Ambassador," as he was termed, was rushed through the maelstrom of acclaim from the luncheon tendered him by the Foreign Minister, Briand, to the Invalides, where he spoke words of cheer to the less fortunate heroes of the World War who had lost arms and legs and eyes in their service to their country.

In the pathetic group of disabled men were aviators whose remade faces showed the price paid for their valiant endeavor. Deeply moved, Captain Lindbergh humbly expressed his admiration for the heroic part these men played, as he shook their hands.

Whirling out of the Champs Élysées into the Place de la Concorde on his way to the Hôtel de Ville, the young aviator passed through throngs of people as the cry, "Voila Lindbergh!" "Brave Lindbergh!" filled the air. Modestly, almost shyly, the hero, who, in America, had feared he would be lonely in Paris, acknowledged the cheers, and, as the volume of sound grew, turned, in his confusion, and engaged in earnest conversation with Ambassador Herrick, obviously embarrassed by the adulation offered him.

THE HEART OF FRANCE BEATS FOR AMERICA

At the Hôtel de Ville eloquent praises for his achievement were offered by Pierre Godin, Paul Bouju, Prefect of Police Chiappe, and M. d'Hercecourl. As they spoke, Lindbergh, holding his gray felt hat in his hand, leaned forward, listening intently. When Mr. Herrick, the American Ambassador, was introduced, there was a wild burst of applause, as though, being an American too, he was entitled to special recognition.

"There are times," said Ambassador Herrick, "when all things improbable seem to be chosen to demonstrate the power of the Creator and to interpret that power. At this moment, when there are misunderstandings and discussions and the real sentiment of the people is obscured through want of understanding or evil intent, France and America needed some such sign, some interpretation of the heart of one people toward the other," he continued.

"Because these manifestations have so impressed me I wonder if this isn't the beginning of a return of that reciprocal understanding.

"This boy can go back and tell, as no other man can, how the heart of France beats for America. By the same token he has brought what can't be brought in diplomatic bags—brought the heart and spirit of America. Not only do you understand, but the people of the streets understand. We—when the boy says 'we' he means his plane and himself, but when I say 'we' I mean the boy and I—we understand and can hardly give expression to the honor you do us today. We appreciate it from the bottom of our hearts and thank you."

When Captain Lindbergh was presented, the applause which had followed the Ambassador's speech increased in volume. He dropped his gray hat, walked to the forum, and spoke with habitual briefness, but with no sign of self-consciousness.

"I am unable to express my appreciation of the honor you have given my country and me since my arrival in France," he began.   "I have but one remaining desire. That is that my flight be the forerunner of a regular air service uniting your country and mine as they have never been united before.   That is my hope today, as I believe M. Bleriot hoped that his flight to England would be the forerunner of the commercial aviation of today.

"I believe if those gallant Frenchmen, Nungesser and Coli"—here he was interrupted by tremendous cheers—"had landed in New York instead of me here in Paris, this would have been their greatest desire."

When the shouts and applause subsided, M. Godin announced that the Grand Medal d'Or of the City of Paris had been voted to Lindbergh and would be presented to him within a short time.

"VIVE LINDBERGH!"

Outside the Hôtel de Ville tens of thousands who had waited patiently for a glimpse of the young hero, broke into wild enthusiasm when he appeared with Ambassador Herrick on the balcony.   In his hand he carried the flags of France and America.   When he left the building, he received the greatest demonstration of the day.   Policemen tried to press back the solid wall of humanity which surged toward him.   But they could not do it.   There was a narrow, tight aisle in which the official automobile stood and received the American boy, the American Ambassador, M. Chiappe, and M.

Godin.   When they were seated, restraint was loosened.   The police could no longer hold the 40,000 persons in the square.   They swept, thousands on thousands, across the square, closing in upon the car, shouting, "Vive Lindbergh!" as they ran with it.

CHAPTER XII

AT five-thirty on Friday morning, Captain Lindbergh astonished the French nation, which is accustomed to spending the dawn warmly tucked in its bed, by going to Le Bourget and taking a spin over the city in the *Spirit of St. Louis*.

Some of the most expert army aviators in France watched his maneuvers from the field. Their astonishment and admiration for his aërial acrobatic skill, which outclassed in daring anything hitherto seen in Paris, was without bounds. Accompanied by Sergeant Detroyat, a French aviator, Lindbergh dipped down and over the Eiffel Tower, shot over the American Embassy, and sped at a high altitude down the Champs Élysées.

The whir of the planes brought sleepy Paris leaping from its bed to watch the soaring of the young American. When rockets were sent off as a signal to the two fliers to descend for breakfast, Sergeant Detroyat obeyed its demand, but the dauntless American, obviously enjoying his brief moment of freedom which preceded a day that was to be packed with social obligations, shot higher into the air, falling first in the "falling leaf," then upward again for an Immelmann turn, and for audacious loops which brought shouts of excitement from the audience below. Reluctantly, he descended at last, to receive high praise from his French comrades and a much needed breakfast.

At nine o'clock he passed through the thronged enthusiastic streets of Paris, and went to the tomb of Napoleon in the Hôtel des Invalides, which was the first of a long series of visits to notable places. At all points, the crowds closed in upon him as tightly as possible, pouring their adulation upon him with roses and by word of mouth.

WELCOMED BY THE PRESIDENT OF FRANCE

He was the guest of Minister of War Painlcvc at luncheon, and immediately afterward visited the French Senate to receive a greeting which equaled that of the historic scene on Wednesday. On the platform in the President's salon the aviator was flanked by President Doumergue, Ambassador Herrick, General Pershing, and General Gouraud. Every inch of space in the huge hall was filled with people eager to add to the tribute which has been his since he arrived in Paris.

President Doumergue welcomed Lindbergh warmly, and presented him with a copy of a resolution which recorded the tribute of the French Senate to him, again pledging "the sympathy and amity which we hold for America." Following an address by Lazare Weiller, who told of the experiments of the Wright brothers, Ambassador Herrick made a comparison between Lindbergh and Lafayette. He declared "Lafayette's inspiration had been to aid the colonies, that he did not come for his government but had executive approval. Lindbergh's inspiration was also his own."

In response the young American reviewed the progress of aviation, sketching the development from
Wright and Bleriot "of a few days ago" to the present
day. Struggling to avoid in his speech any reference
to himself, he blushed furiously when "and I flew from
New York to Paris" slipped out against his will. He
predicted that in ten years airplanes would be flying
regularly over the Atlantic Ocean. The statement
brought thunderous applause from his audience.

THE SURGING CROWDS

With not a moment for relaxation, and with no sign
of fatigue, the stalwart American was dashed from
group to group of enthusiastic committees, each
wanting, in its endeavor, to show him their depth of
admiration. Scarcely given time for his dinner at the
Ministry of War, at which glowing tributes were paid
him by Painleve and Franklin Bouillon, the transatlantic hero was hurried to the gala benefit at the Aëro
Club of France, given to aid the families of dead fliers.
Everywhere he went, crowds surged and jammed the
way, making an effort to see, speak to, or shake hands
with their hero. Throughout the excitement, Captain
Lindbergh maintained his humorous, dignified equilibrium, enviable to those more accustomed to royal
receptions.

The arrival of Lindbergh at the Champs Élysée
Theatre, in an evening dress of faultless cut, which was
very different from the borrowed suit of blue he had
worn earlier in the week, was the signal for a demonstration which brought the 2500 spectators to their
feet in an acclaim which shook the building.

Long before Lindbergh appeared, the theater lobby was jammed. A double row of aces, among whom were D'Oisy, Poli, and Marchetti, made a pathway for the hero. He went immediately to the box occupied by Ambassador Herrick.

The program got under way, after a rousing welcome, when Captain l'Hopital, aide to Marshal Foch, announced in the name of all the French aviators, that they wished to express their thanks to Lindbergh.

AN AUTOGRAPH THAT BROUGHT $1500

The auctioning of Lindbergh's autograph was a feature of the evening. Captain Wylli Coppens, a Belgian ace, conducted the bidding, which started at 1500 francs. It was finally bought by William H. Waters for $1500.

The theater offered a gorgeous spectacle. French and American flags set a background for the beautiful women. The flash of jewels was dimmed by the constant motion of white arms which made a sea of motion whenever the enthusiasm rose in waves. Again and again the program of the evening was stopped when a solitary "bravo" released from hundreds of throats admiration for the quiet boy in the box.

Mary Garden, the beloved American opera singer, dressed as Liberty, sang "The Star-Spangled Banner" and the "Marseillaise," followed by "Carry Me Back to Old Virginny." In the audience were all the members of the American Embassy staff, War Minister Painleve, M. Flandin, president of the Aëro club, various French generals, Mrs. W. K. Vanderbilt,

Clifford B. Harmon, and scores of prominent American and Parisian society.

Approximately 325,000 francs was realized at the entertainment, all of which will go to the unfortunate families of French aviators who lost their lives in their calling.

LINDBERGH'S MESSAGE TO FRANCE

The last thing Lindbergh did before he went to his well-earned rest that night was to give out a statement, expressing his gratitude for the heart-stirring reception from the moment he arrived in France. His concluding words were: "I shall tell the people when I get home, what you have done for me."

The message in full was:

"I will leave France with my ship, the *Spirit of St. Louis*, tomorrow. We came here knowing that we would find friends, but little dreaming how great would be the welcome we have received. I wish it were possible to tell everyone that I will never forget the kindness that has been shown me and I beg the favor of the French press to help me express to the people of France my deepest gratitude.

"All the kindness the French people have shown me and the honors they have bestowed upon me are doubly dear to me as an aviator because France has been the leader in the development of aviation and has filled pages of history with the names of her glorious heroes. Captains Nungesser and Coli tried to cross the Atlantic from east to west, which in my opinion is the hardest way, and, although they did not succeed, their names are immortal. I wish I could stay longer in France, but in leaving I ask the press to give the parting message that I shall never forget the friendship shown me by the people of this glorious country and that I realize that it is not for me alone, but an expression of sentiment the French people have for the land of my birth."

CHAPTER XIII

Farewell, Paris

ALTHOUGH his arduous social duties had kept him up until very late Friday night, the young aviator, whose youth and health as much as anything have been foremost factors in his success, was up at dawn. After his American breakfast of eggs and bacon, he hurried out to Le Bourget to work on his plane so that everything should be in perfect order for his flight to the next step in foreign adventures.

Paris, so loath as a rule to bestir itself until the day is well established, had slept with half-closed eyes, afraid to miss a moment of this, the last glimpse of the hero who had crept so easily and firmly into its heart. It was very early when the streets started to fill with patient, smiling people. A fine day, they told each other, a safe day for the Lone Eagle to start anew on his journey, for the sky was smooth blue and the sun shone down as though it, too, was offering salutation and an assurance of fair weather.

At Le Bourget less than fifty people had been able to gain admission to the hangar where the *Spirit of St. Louis* stood being primed by eager French mechanics who for two days had worked feverishly, bringing it to the pitch of perfection. Those who were lucky enough to see the plane were amazed at its tiny proportions. It looked like a dwarf as it stood beside a great three-motored monoplane, under the wings of which it could easily have passed.

It had been arranged that Lindbergh should give his farewell to Paris in a message wrapped in a French flag at the base of Cleopatra's Needle, the obelisk brought from Egypt by Napoleon in the historic Place de la Concorde. The package was prepared as he ate two sandwiches at 10.45 in the hangar. It was then he discovered that souvenir hunters had made off with the precious pneumatic life raft, his sole reliance had he been forced down on the Atlantic, and two pneumatic cushions. Understanding for the human weakness for souvenirs was in his mood as he smilingly told reporters that no questions would be asked by him if the missing articles were returned.

IN THE AIR AGAIN

After an emotional moment when those who had been with him in closest association during the too short time he had spent in their midst said farewell, Captain Lindbergh climbed into his little wicker chair.

Every precaution had been taken to have a clear field and to avoid the confusion of a crowd such as had menaced his safety the night of his arrival at Le Bourget.

At his request, there was no formal escort. The French government had detailed military planes to go with him to Belgium, but they followed at some distance. As a personal tribute, three planes, headed by Commandant Weiss, a friend of Lindbergh, flanked the military planes.

The take-off of the *Spirit of St. Louis* was perfect.

6

After a moment of tense silence, the little white plane buzzed like a gigantic bee, gliding rapidly northwest across the smooth field, and then, after a run of 150 yards, turned sharply into the air, and mounted at an angle of nearly forty-five degrees. Below him, the little group of close friends watched with moist eyes the valiant white bird with its courageous owner as it soared away.

"GOOD-BY, DEAR PARIS!"

Beyond the field, Paris waited breathlessly for the last look at the American aviator. Slowly, after the first tense moment, when the airplane soared over the mass of humanity which reached for miles along his way, a great roar arose, and was sustained, with the shrill tooting of horns and whistles, until the last faint streak of the *Spirit of St. Louis* disappeared into the sky.

Captain Lindbergh seemed loath to leave the city which had offered him so bountifully of hospitality. He spread his au revoir affectionately over the city. He circled the Arc de Triomphe, in homage to the Unknown Poilu, and then, flying to an altitude of only 200 yards, went twice around the Eiffel Tower.

His amazing mastery of his ship was shown when, true to his appointment, he dove straight at the apex of Cleopatra's Needle and released his flag-inclosed farewell. As it fluttered to earth there was a mad convergence and scramble by spectators. Howard Darring, an American who formerly flew with the Seventy-first French Air Squadron, grasped it first. An unidentified man tore part of the flag and made away with the fragment. The remainder and the good-by written on a letter sheet of the American Embassy were turned over to Raymond Orteig, donor of the New York-to-Paris prize won by Lindbergh.

The message was a throw-back to the flier's Irish ancestors. They said "Cead Mille Failthe," Gaelic for "ten thousand welcomes." He said "ten thousand thanks" in good American. Thus it read:

"Good-by, dear Paris. Ten thousand thanks for your kindness to me.

"CHARLES A. LINDBERGH."

At Senlis, where many Americans were quartered during the World War and where the Mayor had begged that he show himself to the people, he dipped over the town and dropped a tiny American flag.

Again, as in the transatlantic flight, Captain Lindbergh traveled with the minimum of personal equipment. His baggage, which had increased astonishingly since his arrival in Paris, was sent ahead by regular passenger plane so that he would not be obliged to borrow any clothing from the King of Belgium.

"TO THE GLORY OF CHARLES LINDBERGH"

Certainly no individual, with the exception of President Wilson, has ever been the recipient of such laudatory praise and honors as had Captain Lindbergh during his stay in Paris. Each day brought evidence of the love and admiration which the French people bore him. Persons of every rank from the highest state officials, artists, sculptors, poets, actors, and actresses, have shown their eagerness to contribute their bit to his glory.   At a special performance at a theater for the benefit of the families of stricken aviators, an ode "To the glory of Charles Lindbergh" was specially written by Mlle. Jehanne d'Orlian, and declaimed by the famous French actress Cecil Sorel.

The contents of his final address to the French people, which was given out for publication just before he left Paris, made a deep impression.   Its sincerity struck a deep note in the appreciative hearts of the French, not only because of its simplicity, but owing to his generosity in always keeping the names of Nungesser and Coli, the two fateful aviators who had started out to do what he had accomplished, as a beacon before him.

"All the kindness the French people have shown me, and the many honors they have bestowed," he said, "are doubly dear to me as an aviator because France has been a leader in the development of aviation and has filled the pages of history with the names of her glorious heroes."   In his reference to Nungesser and Coli he declared, "theirs was the hardest way across the Atlantic, and although they did not succeed, their names are immortal."

His strength and calmness is another attribute which appeals to the French.   In spite of his arduous duties which would severely tax an older man, he was always alert and ready and eager to go on with the program arranged for him.   Never was there a hint of weariness or boredom.   One of the last things he did, and after a strenuous day filled to the brim with activity, was to insist upon attending a boxing tourney of the Sporting Club of France in aid of the "Phare de

France," the association of war blinded, where the performers were blind British and Frenchmen. He autographed two programs which were auctioned for $320 and consented to the sale of a letter he had written to the Aëro Club of France which brought $1000.

ROSTAND'S POEM: "TO LINDBERGH"

To Maurice Rostand, the celebrated French poet and dramatist, is due the beautiful picture of Lindbergh, "holding in check death, distance, and the solitude." Rostand's poem, "To Lindbergh," written shortly after the arrival of the young aviator at Le Bourget flying field, bears under the title a quotation from Alan Seegar's poem, "I Have a Rendezvous with Death." The poem, translated, follows:

> You had danced all that night,
> And you had left in uncertain light,
> Alike Alan Seeger, but less young than he,
> But poet also.
>
> You had danced all that night,
> And you had left alone at dawn,
> And, seeing you leave thus alone,
> The air still quivers.
>
> And Newfoundland, with heart so young,
> When solitary you passed above,
> Kneeling on the bare sand,
> Sent up a prayer.
>
> You danced all that last day,
> And you left alone when the day broke.
> Your mother wept as she taught,
> But less than her pupils.

And it was with a heart lost in the wind
You braved aloft the salty breeze,
And you lost not a single instant,
Son of Evangeline.

And you flew a day and a half
Above the sea, above the earth;
A day and a half you did not sleep,
Not even a second.

Young traveler, with dream of steel,
Through the dawn and the twilight
Dost know who 'twas that freed you
From that airplane cell?

Dost know who made you, bold young man,
Strike straight for Paris, blindly perhaps,
Which let you, ne'er having seen it,
Recognize the place?

Dost know who let you hold in check
Death, distance and the solitude?
Dost know who caused you to arrive
With such exactitude?

'Twas not the pride of this great feat
Nor the trembling praise of Old Europe,
Nor the white light at Le Bourget turning,
Nor yet your periscope.

Nor was it yet two continents,
Which two days long breathed the same air,
Nor that you sailed at the moment when
You embraced your mother.

'Twas those young men, with hearts so brave,
Who full of fervor and good will,
Came from your home, too soon forgot,
To die for France.

That which had brought you, predestined one,
Through all these risks where others fell,
It was the rendezvous which they gave you
At their fresh graves.

CHAPTER XIV

Lindbergh Meets His First King

TWO hours and twenty-six minutes after Captain Lindbergh left Le Bourget in the *Spirit of St. Louis*, he arrived in Belgium. The great crowd which had gathered early in the morning, despite the fact that it was known he could not reach Brussels until the middle of the afternoon, sighted the shining white monoplane as it soared over the field at 3.12. A volume of cheers went up as it began to swoop downward. An escort of two Belgian army planes had met him at the Franco-Belgian border, and joined, at a respectful distance, the several planes which had come with him from Paris.

CIRCLING THE CITY OF BRUSSELS

Circling the city in an airman's greeting, Lindbergh dipped and rose as the other planes kept their formation about the flying field. Finally, his silver plane shot through the center of the wide circle of escorting planes, and swooped down, settling as gently as a bird upon the field. Although the day had been overcast, and some rain had fallen fitfully, the ground was comparatively dry for landing. For a moment it looked as though the stampede at Le Bourget on the night of his arrival would be repeated, but the police succeeded in checking the rush just as it seemed about to overwhelm the plane and its owner.

The first man to grasp the aviator's hand was James C. Dunn, the American Chargé d'Affaires. Quickly following was Henri Jasper, the Belgian Premier, who welcomed Captain Lindbergh in the name of the government. The band played "The Star-Spangled Banner" as Lindbergh entered an automobile and was driven to the reviewing stand. Meanwhile, the *Spirit of St. Louis* was placed on a high platform where it could be viewed by the crowd without danger to it.

"THE PEOPLE MUST SEE LINDBERGH"

The greatest care was taken by the committee in charge for the protection of the young aviator. That the airdrome and the roads might be kept clear, the entire Brussels garrison was marched out to guard the essential points. "The people must see Lindbergh," was the edict, "but they must be kept from pushing in about him." With the first streak of daylight, the people began to assemble. All kinds came, from every class in the country, men and women afoot, in milk carts, on bicycles, and in motors.

The greatest precaution was taken to keep open the route which would be covered by the aviator in reaching the American Embassy, the tomb of the unknown soldier, and the Royal Palace. But, as in many instances of well-made plans, at the most important instance they went astray. When Lindbergh arrived to place the wreath on the tomb, the crowd forgot what it was expected to do, forgot gendarme and soldier, forgot everything but its desire to pay homage to this miraculous youth. It surged like a gigantic wave, which threatened to engulf the car in which he sat.

Again that luck which has followed him throughout his
life saved him from harm.   The strong arm of the law,
reinforced with carbine butts, batons, and fists, drove
back the turbulent mass, and Lindbergh, under heavy
escort of the American Chargé d'Affaires, was permitted
to lay the magnificent wreath at the foot of the war
memorial column.

As he drove through the town, the acclaim was deafening.   As he passed the palace King Albert and other
members of the royal family appeared at the windows.

TWO FLYING KINGS MEET

Two hours after the arrival of the aviator, the two
flying kings met, when King Albert of Belgium, affectionately called the "Flying King" by his subjects,
because of his love of the sport, met Lindbergh, the
"King of the Fliers."   Queen Elizabeth, also an aviation enthusiast, greeted him and introduced him to the
Duke and Duchess of Brabant, the latter formerly
Princess Astrid of Sweden, and the other members of
the royal household.

It was at six o'clock that Captain Lindbergh arrived
at the palace to be formally welcomed by the King and
Queen of Belgium and "in the name of the Belgian
people both as an aviator and a representative of the
American people."

During this impressive ceremony, surrounded by
the royal family and court officials, the young aviator
stood out vividly in the leather coat and sport suit
in which he had flown from France.   The magnificent
room was heavy with silence as King Albert gravely
pinned on the lapel of the flying coat the coveted cross

of the Knight of the Order of Leopold.   When this
was finished Captain Lindbergh was presented to
Queen Elizabeth, Prince Charles, and Princess Marie
Josephine.   The conversation in English which followed was informal and vivacious, and Captain Lindbergh later expressed his gladness on being able, once
again, to understand all that was said to him.

THE CROWDS OUTSIDE

Outside the royal palace the crowds had grown until
the streets were black with excited human bodies.   A
squad of picked Belgian cavalry, chosen to do double
duty of maintaining order and displaying honor to the
guest, had difficulty in holding back the teeming crowds
which pushed forward to see the young hero.   Cries
of "Bravo, Lindbergh!" and "Long live Lindbergh!"
rose when he appeared on the steps, and followed him
along the route in the automobile to the Belgian Aëro
Club, where he was greeted by Minister of Aviation
Anseele.   After a brief speech lauding Lindbergh for
his achievement, M. Anseele introduced the illustrious
guest to a group of the best known of Belgian fliers.
Following this the Aëro Club gold medal was presented to him.   This was the first time the medal
had ever been given to a foreigner.

During a brief and much needed rest at the American
Embassy, Captain Lindbergh was obliged to respond
to the thousands gathered below the windows.   Cheer-
fully he stepped out on the balcony, accompanied by
Chargé d'Affaires Dunn, and smiled as he waved the
Belgian emblem toward the cheering people below.

As the guest of the American Club at dinner he

responded to the toast of 700 members with a speech which held them spellbound not only on account of its simplicity and straightforwardness, but also the information it contained. An accurate measurement of the gasoline remaining in the Ryan machine, after landing in France, he said, was 45 gallons, enough for another 360 miles.

"A week ago tonight I landed at Le Bourget. When I left New York there were two things I looked forward to. One was arriving in Paris and the other was seeing Belgium. Now I shall be able to return to America with complete satisfaction."

Including the preparations and many incidents previous to the start-off in America, Captain Lindbergh proceeded to review his flight for the guests, who included many American citizens of Brussels and notable Belgians. He declared that commercial aviation was practicable and needed only financial backing, and explained why a single motor and single pilot were chosen for his experiment.

"A single engine is more desirable because of the greater cruising radius than a double motor on account of the weight involved, and a single pilot meant 300 gallons more of gasoline," he concluded.

AN UNCEREMONIOUS VISIT TO THE PLANE

On Sunday King Albert and Queen Elizabeth paid an unceremonious visit to the hangar to see the *Spirit of St. Louis*. Unaccompanied by the usual escort, the democratic rulers of Belgium arrived at the flying field at ten o'clock in the morning. The meeting had been arranged *sub rosa* at Captain Lindbergh's audience at the palace the day before. They were met at the gate by the youthful American, and taken at once to view the little silver plane.

King Albert exclaimed over the ship's beauty, and being himself a veteran of the air, was especially amazed by its lightness.

"Please show me, Captain Lindbergh," he said in English, "that new compass which gave such wonderful results. I am very anxious to see it."

Lindbergh opened the door of the cockpit and explained how the earth-inductor worked and why it helped him so greatly on his flight. The King listened intently, with Queen Elizabeth at his elbow also catching every word.

"And where is the periscope you used?" the King wanted to know.

The youth explained its position and the manner in which it solved the problem of forward vision so he could carry more fuel.

King Albert closely examined the entire control board, tested the levers, and admired the compactness with which everything was arranged. Then he asked:

"Where do you carry so much fuel?"

"Well, you see, Your Majesty," the flier replied, "everything is arranged with perfect balance. The tanks are placed here and there, and by flying alone I was able to fill them to the limit."

Lindbergh invited the King to sit in the cockpit and the ruler immediately climbed into the famous wicker chair. He released the levers, examined the instrument board and finally said:

"It is a splendid ship. I am not surprised by your great success."

Lindbergh glowed with pride. As the King climbed down Lindbergh turned to the Queen and almost shyly asked:

"Would Your Majesty also like to sit in the plane?"

Queen Elizabeth's reply left no doubt as to her desire. "I should like it very much indeed," she said.

So the "King of the Air" handed the Queen of the Belgians into the tiny compartment and again pointed out the most interesting features, as Belgian air pilots who had approached in the meantime watched, delighted.

THE QUEEN PHOTOGRAPHS THE LONE EAGLE

As the royal couple were about to leave, the Queen remembered something. Turning to Lindbergh, she said:

"I want to take your picture by your plane. Now won't you stand there beside it with the King?"

Lindbergh blushed and bowed, and then smiling took a position with King Albert, while the Queen extracted a tiny camera, focused it on them and carefully clicked the shutter.

The King and Queen then went with Lindbergh and the Belgian pilots to the hangars where were planes recently flown by Belgian officers, Medatz and Ver Halgen. While viewing these machines the Queen again turned to Captain Lindbergh and said, "I must have another picture of the Captain." She directed the pilots to stand with him, and snapped another souvenir of the visit. Captain Lindbergh expressed his admiration for the knowledge which the King of Belgium showed concerning aviation. When the royal visitors had gone, he declared, "The King showed the greatest enthusiasm for aviation and knows all about it. Both he and the Queen were tremendously interested in everything aboard my ship."

This friendly interlude occurred just after Lindbergh had received a delegation of the Automobile Club, and had been presented with a beautiful bronze called "The Spirit of Speed," by Pierre de Hoete, a famous sculptor, who made the presentation himself. Following this ceremony, Captain Lindbergh motored to Bellevue Palace for an unofficial visit with Crown Prince Leopold, who had been his companion at dinner the night before, and the Crown Princess, the former Princess Astrid of Sweden. Ten thousand Belgians, who had been waiting for hours along the route, cheered wildly as the airman and Mr. Dunn moved through the street in their motor.

At City Hall, Burgomaster Max, the war-time hero, welcomed the flier and declared his flight was "an act which will start a new phase in the history of the world."

THE BURGOMASTER SAYS "BRAVO!"

"Dear Captain Lindbergh," he said, "I should like to welcome you in your own language. No doubt I shall make many mistakes, and my pronunciation will be far from good, but I trust you will excuse and understand me. In this City Hall, where I have had the honor to receive so many great and illustrious men, I am proud to salute a real hero.

"The best which you have accomplished and which

immediately created around your name world-wide celebrity is not only wonderful sporting performance showing your remarkable sangfroid courage. It was also an act which will start a new phase in the history of the world. Precisely because this nonstop flight from New York to Paris appeared to be an undertaking beyond human forces, your victory is the victory of humanity.

"In your glory, there is glory for all men. An apparently impossible task loomed before you. You surmounted it. It is helpful and encouraging for those who think we must never despair of human effort. You must have heard many times during these last days that in crossing the ocean with your *Spirit of St. Louis* you have done more than all the diplomats to bring closer together the different peoples. I repeat it myself.

"When a statement is being commonly used, a burgomaster should not hesitate to express it again, as his function when he speaks is to reflect public opinion.

"In uniting by airway your young country with the old soil of Europe you have drawn nearer together these two continents and you have the right to claim the title of citizen of the world. The way now opens; others will follow you, as others tried in vain to precede you.

"I am thus certain, as we welcome you here, to express your own sentiment in mentioning with emotion the names of Nungesser and Coli, who a few days ago, with an assurance as great as yours, started over the Atlantic but never reached their goal.

"Seeing in you the symbol of daring," he continued as Lindbergh nodded his head in response, "and courage, it is impossible for me not to admire your modesty and simplicity. Heroes always consider what they have done a simple matter. This is precisely because they are heroes.

"I salute in you, dear Captain Lindbergh, a noble son of your great nation, which at an hour when civilization was in danger came to its help, and with us conquered."

Then, amid applause, Burgomaster Max, in real American fashion, called, "Three cheers for Captain Lindbergh."

Captain Lindbergh responded: "This afternoon I must leave Belgium. I wish I might stay for days or weeks and get to know better your people. But it is necessary to proceed back to America. No matter where I go, I can never forget Belgium and France. I want to thank you for the great honors I have received here. As I said before, I wish I could stay longer."

FINAL SCENES IN BELGIUM

At the conclusion of his speech the aviator received from Burgomaster Max a gold medal in the name of the city of Brussels. It was inscribed, "Captain Charles A. Lindbergh, the City of Brussels, May 29, 1927." The flier stood at attention as M. Bouillez, the baritone from the Belgian Opera House, sang "The Star-Spangled Banner." At the finish Lindbergh congratulated him and asked him to sing "La Braban-çonne," the Belgian national anthem. He declared he had heard the music many times upon his trip, but never the words. His request brought a burst of frantic

7

approval from the crowd, which became silent only when the artist began singing.

Before he left the building Captain Lindbergh was escorted to the flag-draped balcony and stood bareheaded while the multitude cheered.

After a luncheon at the American Embassy, he hurried to the air field and immediately inspected his machine for his second flight across water to England. He donned his leather coat, said good-by to those who were with him, and stepped into the plane. Preceded by five army planes as an escort of honor, he started toward the channel. At Wargehen, a short space from Brussels, where American soldiers are buried, he made three circles, then, shutting off the engine, dived down to drop a wreath upon a doughboy's grave.

CHAPTER XV

THE EAGLE VISITS THE LION

PARISIAN and Belgian crowds had amazed Captain Lindbergh, but he was utterly unprepared for the mass of 150,000 men and women who surged across the landing field at Croydon Aërodrome to welcome him when he landed in England. The police, as well, were overwhelmed by the human avalanche which swept everything aside and surged ahead, plowing down fences and the hand of the law in its desire to greet the "Lone Eagle."

At 3.31 P. M. Captain Lindbergh left Brussels in the *Spirit of St. Louis* and was first seen over Dunkirk at 4.40 P. M. The heart of London had its first glimpse of the eaglet as he avoided the usual cross-channel route and flew along the Kentish coast and up the Thames Valley. When he reached the aërodrome at 6 P. M. the solid sea of faces turned up to him made him decide to climb skyward again until order had cleared a safe place in which to bring down his beloved plane.

"THERE HE IS!"

The crowds had begun to gather early in the morning, although it was known that the American could not reach the aviation field until late afternoon. By three o'clock the field, which is nearly four miles in circumference, was outlined by a human band of enormous thickness.   The air was alive with agitated American flags of all sizes.   Order was maintained with ease until the approaching hour of six loosened all restraint.   At ten minutes of the hour several large, black specks were seen against the intense blue of the English sky.

"There he is!" screamed a hundred thousand voices, and each body pushed forward to be nearer its objective. Ropes gave way like thin twine, fences fell like toothpicks, and the 1200 policemen had the force of midgets before an army of giants.

All the plans and details which had been carefully made for the reception of the *Spirit of St. Louis* and its fearless owner were swept into nothingness by the gigantic human "tank" which swept ruthlessly on its way.   The specks which had been seen were the planes of the escort which accompanied Lindbergh. With him they circled the aërodrome.   At last the silver monoplane, shimmering like a sea gull, started to descend.

A great roar rose from the thousands of voices, and once again the human wave deluged the field.   Like a timid bird, the *Spirit of St. Louis* turned skyward again, for the man in it, whose one worry since he arrived on foreign soil was for the safety of his plane, was fearful for it.

The officials below threatened and beat back the crowd, which, when it realized its hero would not come down until he could land with security, slowly gave way, and once more the famous airplane fluttered down to rest on English soil.

Every effort was made to protect Captain Lindbergh, but for a few moments it appeared as though human

© *Pacific and Atlantic Photos*

BRUSSELS WELCOMES LINDBERGH

The "Ace of the Atlantic" responds to the greeting of the huge crowd in the street from the

A ROYAL PHOTOGRAPHER

Captain Lindbergh poses for Queen Elizabeth of Belgium in a group including King Albert at the flier's left

endeavor would be worsted by superhuman activity. The moment the silver plane touched the earth the tidal wave broke over it. The reception committee was swept to one side and for a time it looked as though the gallant aviator would be completely submerged. Commander Perrin, secretary of the Royal Aëro Club, and other officials used strong-arm methods which were finally effective. But it was not until a rope had been stretched a safe distance from the plane, shutting off the exuberant people, that Captain Lindbergh left the plane.

THE HUMAN CHAIN OF POLICEMEN

As he locked the door to the cockpit he said, "Look after my machine." The words were enough. A human chain of policemen, joined hand to hand, formed about the precious structure, and at the risk of their lives established an impregnable wall of protection.

This demonstration was only a prelude to that which met and followed him from the moment he stepped into the motor car with Commander Perrin and was driven to the air-buildings for safety. Men, women, and children clamored for a word from the young aviator. Commander Perrin, looking like a veritable John Bull, entered the control tower and, shouting through the megaphone, reminded the people that the Royal Aëro Club had promised nothing further than a sight of the airman, and that, until they went home, he could not get away.

"WORSE THAN PARIS"

"Speech! Speech! Lindbergh! Lindbergh!" rose in waves from the excited crowd. Finally, with a pleasant smile, Captain Lindbergh climbed up the ladder, and taking the megaphone, said, "I just want to tell you this is worse than I had in Paris." The people went mad with delight, and those on the far side of the tower yelled their demand to hear as well. Walking to the other side, the airman called out, "I've just said this is a little worse than Le Bourget, or, I should say, better."

When he tried to descend the enthusiastic Americans and English imperiled their hero with too great a demonstration, and he was obliged to run up the ladder again to avoid extinction.

A way was finally wedged for Ambassador Houghton's car to approach the tower to take the guest to London. The Ambassador and his staff were already seated, and each time Captain Lindberg started down the ladder the people rushed at him. He was finally obliged to make a flying leap to the seat of safety in the car. So great was the pressure against the window of the car that the glass was smashed into fragments.

The reception committee, which had been swept in all directions by the crush of the multitudes, was finally collected. Among them were the counselor of the English Embassy, Frederick Sterling, the British Air Minister, and Lady Hoare. After greetings had been exchanged, the police made desperate efforts to get Ambassador Houghton's car to the building. On its arrival Captain Lindbergh made a direct appeal to the people through the megaphone. "The Ambassador wants me to ask you to please clear a way for his car— he asks me and I am telling you—so we can get out."

The simple request, accompanied by the engaging

smile, touched the crowd, which immediately, but slowly, divided to make way for the hero.

The first thought of the young aviator the next morning was for his plane, and before his hosts were awake he slipped from the house and motored to Croydon Aërodrome, where the *Spirit of St. Louis* was being carefully watched by experts. He found, to his delight, that it was only slightly damaged.

"They hardly touched a thing," he said, "just a little of the tail and wing fabric is torn—but that is nothing at all. When I saw the crowd yesterday I thought they would take the whole lot as a souvenir, but it's O. K."

LONDON "LINDBERGH MAD"

During the day, London became "Lindbergh mad." There was little talk of anything else. Never before had anything vied with the popularity and interest in the Derby, which is the big yearly event in England. But this year it lost out by the coming of the American hero. The flier became overnight the great sensation, and throughout the city groups started early in the day to pay homage to his youth and bravery.

After making sure of his plane's safety, Captain Lindbergh returned to the Embassy and later participated in the London American colony's celebration of Memorial Day. At the Morgan House, where he made a brief speech, Lindbergh emphatically denied any intention of flying back to America. "As a matter of fact," he said, "I would greatly prefer it to a sea trip, because, although I am airworthy, I am not sure of my qualities on the sea."

In the evening, on rounding out one of the busiest days he had had since he left America, Captain Lindbergh was a guest at a banquet given by the Association of American Correspondents in the Abraham Lincoln room of the Savoy Hotel. In front of him was a plate of luscious ham sandwiches and a jug of water, a reminder of his frugal repast during those thirty-three hours when he flew to Paris from America. When he saw the sandwiches, he blushed like a schoolboy and laughed heartily. His one regret was that the plate was swiftly removed before he could touch its fare and a lavish menu substituted. But he was permitted to keep the ice water, the first water with ice which he had had since he left his country.

THE GIFT OF THE PAGE BOYS

As Captain Lindbergh left the hotel at 9 o'clock to enable Ambassador Houghton to catch the *Leviathan* at Southampton and also provide a good night's sleep for the young aviator, two page boys approached him with a salver on which was a package. Inscribed upon the card were the words, "From twenty-four page boys, wishing you the best of luck. And we hope some day one of us may follow your example." On opening the package Captain Lindbergh found a typical boy's gift—a sturdy Scout's knife with numerous devices. The youthful aviator was deeply touched, and his emotion turned to mirth when one of the pages asked him for a halfpenny, following an old custom, in exchange for the gift.

CHAPTER XVI

ENGLAND HONORS THE HERO

WITH all the vigor of youth, Captain Lindbergh was up the next morning at ten minutes of four. The Embassy, unaccustomed to doing with less than the proverbial eight hours' sleep, was thrown into a state of consternation when it knew the young American was up for the day and ready for breakfast. His plane, again, was his objective. After eating heartily, he took a motor car to Croydon Field and at 5.50 A. M. was flying to Gosport, where the *Spirit of St. Louis* was left to be dismantled preparatory to shipment on the United States cruiser *Memphis* for America.

Leaving many instructions for the safe packing of his plane, Lindbergh left for Croydon in a single-seater *Woodcock*, and, with the instinct of a homing pigeon, found the field with an accuracy which astonished the English aviators and pilots who awaited him.

There was just time to make a hasty trip back to the Embassy to change his clothes before he left for his appointment at Buckingham Palace to meet the King of England. Wearing a blue suit, soft white collar, dark tie, and soft hat, he arrived at the palace at 10.45.

On the way to the Palace Captain Lindbergh stopped for a moment at 10 Downing Street to shake hands with Prime Minister and Mrs. Baldwin. They stood talking in the garden as he was leaving the house, and watched for a moment the rehearsal of the beautiful ceremony of the trooping of colors taking place on the historic Horse Guards parade ground.

THE "LONE EAGLE" CONVERSES WITH KING GEORGE

The meeting between the young American and King George was informal in the extreme, and Captain Lindbergh was amazed by the straightforward and democratic attitude of England's monarch. For a half hour the two men were engaged in earnest conversation. The King congratulated him warmly on the amazing feat which he had accomplished and asked many questions regarding the plane and the conditions of the flight. Toward the end of the half hour, during which Captain Lindbergh had been invited to sit as he talked to the sovereign of England, Queen Mary entered the King's private room and, following the presentation of the "Lone Eagle," fell into easy conversation with him.

Before the audience with the King and Queen was ended, King George presented the flier with the rare Air Force Cross, which had only once before been given to a foreigner, when it was bestowed upon the American crew of the NC-4.

As Lindbergh was leaving the palace he met Princess Elizabeth, the youngest member of the royal house, the little daughter of the Duke and Duchess of York, who was patiently waiting in her nurse's arms to see the American hero. After shaking hands formally with her, he stooped and talked, and, as he arose, patted her cheek, while she gazed with delight into his face.

A CHAT WITH THE PRINCE OF WALES

From the palace, Captain Lindbergh went to York House to call upon the Prince of Wales. It was nearly eleven-thirty when the most popular young men in the world met and shook hands. The interview with the Prince was on the usual lines of congratulation, questions, which showed a thorough knowledge of what Captain Lindbergh had accomplished, and an intense interest in all things pertaining to aviation. When questioned, later, as to what he had talked about with the Prince of Wales, Lindbergh, with a broad smile responded, "Oh, about ten minutes."

The American Embassy was the next step in the long program of the day, when he met the staff and many Americans who had called to see him. At one o'clock he was the guest of honor at a luncheon in the Claridge Hotel given by the British Air Council.

Sir Samuel Hoare, Secretary of the Air Council, the chief speaker, declared that Captain Lindbergh's flight had placed him in the foremost rank of pioneers of the air.

LONG-DISTANCE FLIGHTS STIMULATE PROGRESS

"There are some foolish people," he said—"I am glad to think there are very few of them—who are asking the question: 'Of what use to the world are these efforts and sacrifices? What use to the world is a flight like Captain Lindbergh's?' If I had time I could prove to them that from the technical point of view these long-distance flights are of great value. They stimulate progress; they test reliability.

"Is it not of value to the technical progress of aviation that a single air-cooled engine of 220 horsepower, consuming only ten gallons of petrol an hour, should have traveled over 3500 miles and been fit for another lap at the end of it?

"Is not a long-distance flight of this kind of great value as a test of aërial navigation?

"Flying through fogs and storms, Captain Lindbergh never seems to have been deflected from his course. Surely this experience is not only a testimony to his great skill as a navigator, but also a lesson of value in the study of aërial navigation.

"But I set aside these technical justifications, for a flight of this kind the world at large rightly reaches its verdict upon broader grounds. The peoples of many countries are today applauding Captain Lindbergh's achievement not so much because some material gain will be obtained in this or that way, but because it is a fine example of nerve and endurance, of skill, courage, enterprise, and adventure.

"The more drab the world becomes the more gladly we welcome such fine achievements as his.

"Today, therefore, I ask you to drink to the health of Captain Lindbergh as the pilot who has broken the world's record and as a worthy representative of our close friends and war allies, the pilots of the United States of America. Still more, however, do I ask you to drink to his health as a young man who embodies the spirit of adventure and lights up the world with a flash of courage and daring, and, I am glad to say, of success."

When Captain Lindbergh arose to respond to these

ENGLAND'S GREETING TO LINDBERGH

The *Spirit of St. Louis* circling Croydon Airport seeking a place to
land while a hundred thousand Britons wait to welcome him.

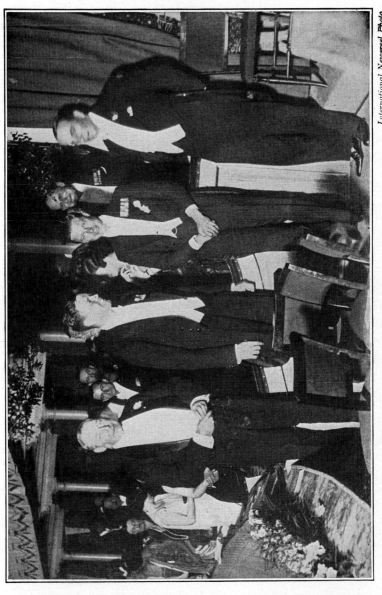

THE PRINCE OF THE AIR AND THE PRINCE OF WALES

Captain Lindbergh standing between the Prince of Wales and Lord Lonsdale in the royal box at the Derby Ball in London

words of Sir Samuel, the 500 guests sat forward breathlessly as he recounted the history of his flight.

THE MACHINE FOR THE FLIGHT

"I will try to give you a short description, from the
standpoint of navigation, of my flight," Lindbergh
said.   "Three and a half months ago a group in St.
Louis decided to construct a plane for the New York-
Paris flight.   Two months later that machine had
been built and tested.   A monoplane type was chosen
instead of a biplane, because of the greater range of a
monoplane on the same amount of petrol.

"The question as to whether to carry a navigator or
second pilot was decided solely because the single pilot
would allow 300 more miles range to the plane.   The
fact that I reached the coast line of Ireland three miles
from the point I was steering for was due to a coincidence.   An error of twenty-five miles was calculated
for in my navigational reckoning.   But if the wind
had drifted us 300 miles out of our course, I still
should have been able to reach Paris, and had I gone
wrong and wound up in Sweden or Spain there would
have been no danger to myself and the plane, although
I couldn't have reached Le Bourget.

WEATHER REPORTS UNSATISFACTORY

"We decided the plane should fly the Great Circle
course, because this saved hundreds of miles in distance.   The observation as to weather conditions was
insufficient.   There was a station in South Greenland,
two or three in Newfoundland, a few ships in the
northern steamer lanes and two or three vessels north

of these. By the reports we got on the night before
we started, the chart showed showers to be met over
Nova Scotia, local storm areas and fog over Newfoundland, but clear weather with high pressure over the
whole North Atlantic route.

"After the take-off at Roosevelt Field, haze conditions were better than expected until night. We met
a slight fog over Nova Scotia and flew through cloud-
bursts and much local rain between Nova Scotia and
Newfoundland. We passed over some ice, too. There
was some fog until we hit Newfoundland but it was
clear from there to 100 miles out at sea.

STORM CLOUDS 15,000 FEET UP

"Then we hit an uncalculated storm area that lasted
all night and much of the following morning. I had
to climb to 8000 feet to get over the storm, as it was
so cold that sleet began forming on the fuselage.
Before morning I had to go up to 10,000 feet. Late
at night the moon came out, but just before morning
we ran into storm clouds that seemed to extend 15,000
feet. They were too high to climb over, so we had to
turn back and run out of the storms. At daybreak we
had to go down through the clouds almost to the surface. Fortunately by this time the temperature had
risen, so there was no ice forming on the plane. From
here on for several hours there was a ceiling of only two
or three hundred feet. For several hours I had to fly
through a dense fog, entirely blind. I couldn't see either
the sky or sea and had to plug along with the aid of my
instruments alone.

"These conditions were entirely contrary to weather

forecasts.   Several hours out on the other side of Ireland I ran into local storms, but there was no fog.

"In the night I saw several light spots in the fog, apparently caused by the lights of ships, but I couldn't make sure.   I did see one ship clearly.   That was early in the night.   From then on I didn't see one until seventy-five or a hundred miles off Ireland, when we passed several fishing smacks.

"One of the most curious features of the trip was a series of mirages I saw several hours out of Ireland. I could see islands and trees and was almost certain it was land, but as I flew on there was nothing but fog and clouds of black, purple, and white that looked like a shore line.   After passing the Irish coast we met no more fog and stormy weather. ' The weather was comparatively clear from then on.

"In conclusion, I want to say that there is nothing secret about our instruments or the plane or anything at all.   I should be happy to give any of you flying men at any time any technical details that I can."

The only time he showed the least embarrassment was when listening to the laudatory eloquence of Brigadier General Lord Thomson, Chairman of the Royal Aëro Club.   "Aside from the magnificent flight, what really appeals to us is the personality of Captain Lindbergh," he said.   "He is a man in every sense of the word, although only twenty-five years old.   He is a fully developed man and what is more he is a modest young man.   That, after all, is really a miracle. One gets vainer as he grows older, but this young man has been exposed to the full blast of the greatest publicity ever directed at any one human being in recent times.   If you would get inside his charming smile, inside his head, you would find a man whose sole desire is to do everything he can to advance aviation."

At the end of the speeches, Captain Lindbergh was presented with the *Daily Mail* gold aviation cup, instituted by Lord Northcliffe.

A TRIBUTE NEVER BEFORE OFFERED TO AN AMERICAN

At four o'clock an ovation was accorded him at the House of Commons by the whole membership.   The members of Parliament gave him a tribute never before offered to an American.   He was the guest of Lord and Lady Astor, and upon his arrival was received by the speaker and escorted to the distinguished strangers' gallery.   After listening to the debate for a few moments, Lindbergh left, while the entire House stood in a body until he had disappeared.   Outside on the terrace he shook hands with members and talked for a short time with Winston Churchill, Chancellor of the Exchequer.

At the House of Lords the young man was greeted with another enthusiastic reception from the older Parliamentarians.

Following the receptions, Lady Astor entertained the aviator at tea on the terrace, officially opening, at the same time, the strawberry and cream season. Strawberries picked at Kent in the morning were served to the airman and other guests, who included distinguished leaders of all political parties and the lobby correspondents.   Lady Astor's only regret was that there was not sufficient time to arrange a dinner for, as she expressed it, "the greatest boy ever."

Captain Lindbergh made a striking figure as he walked about, overtowering Lord Astor, who is by no means short. His simplicity and charm were felt by all who came in contact with him. He wore the ribbon of the Legion of Honor in the lapel of his coat.

The night was a round of feverish activity, beginning with a large dinner at the Hotel Savoy arranged by the Royal Aëro Club and other aëro clubs in Great Britain.

The guests included a long list of distinguished persons, among them the Marquis of Leaming, Winston Churchill, Lord Queensborough, Baron Shaw, Lord of Appeal; Sir Rowland Blades, Lord Mayor of London; Gordon Selfridge, Viscount Cave, Viscount Astor, Canon Carnegie, Lord Thomson, Sir Sefton Brancher, Major H. I. Seagraves, noted auto racer; Sir Alan Cobham, England's premier long-distance flier; T. P. O'Connor, and Lieutenant Colonel W. A. Bishop, famous Canadian flying ace, who won the Victoria Cross, the D. S. O., and the Military Cross in the World War.

Sir Samuel Hoare, proposing Captain Lindbergh's health, pictured a voyage of the future Pilgrim Fathers, saying "that the future *Mayflower* might be an airplane or an airship bearing the name perhaps of Lindbergh, for that name goes down in history.

"The easier communication became between America and Great Britain," he said, "the better it would be for all concerned. Captain Lindbergh arrived as a great aviator; he will leave as an old friend of England's. That is perhaps as important as the achievement of his flight."

Captain Lindbergh responded by thanking England for her enthusiastic welcome, and declared he was looking forward to his return in the near future. Neither the Britons nor the Americans, he said, should lose sight of Sir Alan Cobham's accomplishments or those of Sir Keith Smith, who made a flight to South America in 1919. Nor should they forget the "courage of the daring aviators in the war, whose feats have no parallel in peace-time aviation."

Winston Churchill declared there was not a man, woman, or child in all Britain whose imagination had not been stirred by Lindbergh's air voyage.

LINDBERGH REPRESENTS THE IDEAL MAN

"We all flew his flight in our minds," said the Chancellor, "and felt proud with him of honors bestowed justly wherever he has gone. We have seen too little of him here; he has seen too little of us. We have derived the impression that he represents all a man should say, should do, and should be."

At 10.30 he left with the Swedish Minister for the Mayfair Hotel, where a Swedish festival was in progress in his honor. From the Mayfair he went to the famous Derby eve ball at Albert Hall, where the feminine youth of London awaited its chance to meet and dance with the young aviator. When the word was given that Captain Lindbergh did not dance there was a distinct air of disappointment throughout the assembly.

For the first time in the history of the English Derby, the great sports event of the year did not hold the center of the stage. At Epsom, where the race took place, Captain Lindbergh was the guest of Lord Lonsdale, and was introduced while there to the Duke of Connaught, Lord Londonderry, Lord Sefton, and many other celebrities, who in high silk hats and formal morning suits gave the function an air of exclusiveness and smartness.

Besides being presented to the élite of England, Captain Lindbergh also was introduced to the idiom of the race track. When someone asked him if he had "a little flutter," the airman looked puzzled and repeated the word.

GETTING ACQUAINTED WITH THE RACE TRACK

"That means, did you have a bet?" was the reply to his interrogation.

"Oh, I thought it was something to do with the heart," laughed the American. "We have strange terms in aëronautics, but racing seems to have it beaten."

While he watched the races, it could be seen that this kind of sport did not particularly interest him. Now and then he used the binoculars, but those sharp, well-trained eyes, which had served him so well in flying, did not need the aid of the glasses. When the big event of the day happened, and "Call Boy" went past the post, Captain Lindbergh accepted it as a matter of course, while the English in the paddock and on the stands went wild with enthusiasm. The people, however, seemed to interest him enormously. It was perhaps the largest crowd he had ever seen, notwithstanding the ones which had met him at

Le Bourget and at Croydon. Every foot of space
for miles was filled with eager people.

When asked how he liked the Derby, his response
was, "It was very interesting," but admitted that he
had not bet because he did not know anything about
horse racing.

In the evening Captain Lindbergh was the guest of
honor of his fellow countrymen, when the American
Society in London, the American Chamber of Commerce, and the American Club gave a dinner to him
at the Hotel Savoy. With ease and modesty Captain
Lindbergh expressed the belief that aviation ultimately
would break down the barrier between nations. He
paid tribute to the courage and foresight of the Wright
brothers, Louis Bleriot, who flew across the channel in
1909, and Sir Arthur Britten Brown, who, with the
late Sir John Alcock, flew across the Atlantic. Winston
Churchill, whose mother was also an American, also
spoke as did the Marquis of Reading, who pleaded for
coöperation among the English-speaking nations as the
best means of avoiding conflicts in the future.

CHAPTER XVII

Farewell, England; Back Again, France!

ON Wednesday Captain Lindbergh accepted the invitation of President Coolidge to return to America on the United States cruiser *Memphis*, flagship of Vice-Admiral Guy H. Burrage, Commander of United States naval forces in Europe. The invitation was cabled to the young airman by the special committee of four Cabinet members appointed by President Coolidge for the national celebration in honor of the aviator. By increasing the speed of the *Memphis* from twenty to twenty-five knots an hour, the trip from Cherbourg to Washington could be made in seven days. Arrangements were also made for the transportation of the *Spirit of St. Louis* upon the *Memphis*, so that the beloved plane could be near its owner and assembled for his use the moment he stepped on American soil.

On the day of his departure from London, Captain Lindbergh remained quietly at the American Embassy disposing of private affairs and resting. He lunched with Mrs. Houghton and Miss Matilda Houghton and a few members of the embassy staff.

Before leaving London he wrote a letter of thanks for the reception given him by British aviation bodies during his stay there. The letter, written from the American Embassy, was addressed to Hon. William F. Forbes-Sempill, chairman of the Royal Aëronautical Society. It follows:

"DEAR COLONEL FORBES-SEMPILL:

"I am writing you, as chairman of the Aëronautical Society, in an endeavor to express my thanks for the overwhelming and generous reception I have received from those interested in aëronautics in England.

"Through you and the governing council of the Royal Aëronautical Society I should like to take this opportunity of thanking not only the society, but those other bodies which together govern the field of British aëronautics—the Royal Aëro Club, the Air League of the British Empire, and the Society of British Aircraft Constructors. All four bodies have shown such great interest in my all too brief stay in this country that I feel convinced that the bond of aviation is binding Great Britain and America more closely together than ever before and that it will strengthen with the years to come.

"The spontaneous sincerity of your welcome makes me hope that in the not very distant future I may be able to revisit your country and renew the all too brief acquaintanceships.

"Yours sincerely,
"C. A. LINDBERGH."

At two o'clock he said good-by to his hostess and started for the Kenley airdrome, where a crack British plane was waiting for him to take the controls for his aërial trip of farewell to France.

LINDBERGH PROMISES TO RETURN

"I'll come back and do my sight-seeing later," he said as he took his leave of many friends at the Embassy who had entertained him so cordially during his stay in the British capital.

On his way to Kenley, Captain Lindbergh stopped at Croydon air field, where he was presented with a silver salver by Imperial Airway Pilots. It was engraved with the names of twelve pilot donors and inscribed: "In Commemoration of the great flight from New York to Paris."

At Kenley the mist which had lain upon the land since early morning developed into a thick haze. Over the channel a heavy fog had developed, and reports of a heavy rain were issued from Paris. At four o'clock, an hour after the scheduled start, British pilots declared that the weather was much too risky for the flight. Reluctantly Captain Lindbergh decided to postpone his trip until weather conditions were more favorable.

It was a difficult moment for the British Air Force authorities at Kenley while they waited fearfully for the decision of the intrepid American. At Le Bourget there was the crowd of friends and well-wishers who had been waiting for hours for news of his departure from England. Hundreds of enthusiasts were waiting in the rain for him, hoping he could come in spite of the weather, while hundreds in England were standing in fear and trembling for fear he would go.

READY TO CROSS THE CHANNEL

The single-seater Gloucester *Gamecock* which was to carry him across the channel was primed for the trip. Behind the cockpit a new felt hat, his suitcase, and a parachute were safely packed. Two trim, proud youths from the British Air Force, Flight Lieutenant Boret, and Flying Officer Horimen of the Thirty-second Squadron, were ready to accompany him as far as the coast. Like blooded horses, pawing the ground to be off, the escort, the plane, and the young American were eager to go, while the older element and those responsible for the safety, while on English soil, of the fearless youth, were standing in fear and trepidation, unable, they knew, to cope with the decision to go, once it was made. But the steady, cautious element which had done so much to further the success of the young aviator, came happily to the surface. As the mist thickened he, too, realized the impracticability of a flight against such odds. There was a deep breath of relief from the officers and members of the committee when Captain Lindbergh finally said he would put off going until conditions were more favorable.

As compensation for his disappointment, it was suggested that he might like to take a flip in the *Gamecock* around the field, but Wing Commander Brock, remembering the joyous cavorting of Lindbergh when he tumbled and rollicked like a child over Paris one early morning, and realizing the danger of permitting the lad even a moment's freedom in the tricky weather, quickly announced that this was a decision within his province, and now that the young airman had decided not to go to Paris, there was not the slightest possibility of his being permitted to take any risk for entertainment or relaxation. So, instead of flying, he went cheerfully off to tea with the officers and spent the long hours of waiting among men who talked his language of aëronautics and to whom he was as much a hero as he was to the crowds who waited in the dripping rain at Le Bourget.

At 6.30 A. M. the following morning Captain Lindbergh shook hands all round and stepped into the Gloucester *Gamecock* for the trip across the channel. The weather was not good, and at Lympne, fifty miles from Kenley, he was obliged to descend. Little by little the haze lifted, and as the warming rays of the sun dissipated it almost entirely, the flier once more took to the air at 8.13. Some fog persisted over the channel, but conditions became better as he proceeded, and he landed gracefully on Le Bourget field, the scene of his greatest triumph, at 10.02. He maintained a high altitude throughout the flight over the city, and the thousands who had hoped to see him from their windows were disappointed.

Captain Richard D. White, naval attaché representing the American Embassy, was the first to greet him. The second man to clasp his hand was Benjamin Mahoney, president of the Ryan firm which had built the *Spirit of St. Louis*. The American had been in the airdrome since dawn, and in spite of the cold and damp had waited with eyes turned to the sky for the first glimpse of the famous youth. The greeting between the two Americans was a joyful one. They clasped hands and congratulated each other on the success of the transatlantic flight. Meanwhile the crowd, which had waited for a sight of the young man who had attained the worship of a patron saint, stood patiently back, aware that something deeper than casual acquaintance demanded isolation for the aviator and his friend. But when Lindbergh finally turned to make his way to the motor which was to carry him again to the Embassy the repressed enthusiasm was loosened and he was deluged with the warmth of their emotional appreciation.

At luncheon, 300 aviators were his hosts. The tables were set under the trees of the Bois de Boulogne, near the Clos Norman club house of the international League of which Colonel Clifford B. Harmon, formerly of Philadelphia, is president. Most of the men present had fought in the air during the war, and a number served with the American Lafayette Escadrille. Dr. Edmund L. Gros, chief organizer of the escadrille, in the name of his comrades, presented Lindbergh with a medal and pin of the squadron. He told of the mothers of two French aviators killed in the war watching Captain Lindbergh in his flight to Paris. One weeping, said to the other, "It is as though the spirit of our lost sons were returning to us."

In reply, Captain Lindbergh declared the medal and the pin were "of more value to me than almost any honor I have received in Europe." He spoke modestly of his achievement and again took the occasion to praise the pioneers in the work of aviation. Colonel Harmon commissioned Captain Lindbergh to take the League's gold medal to President Coolidge. The others who have received it are King Albert of Belgium and King Alfonso of Spain.

As a happy omen the sun suddenly burst forth after four days of rain, and the people of Paris turned happily to one another, assured that the young airman had been especially favored by this sign of the gods.

The aviator was received later in the day by Count

Ehrensward, Swedish Minister to France. An audience of Swedish children was in the balcony of the gymnasium, where the exercises in his honor were held, and he was presented, by the children, with masses of flowers. He assured the Swedish Minister that he would "certainly go to Sweden" when he returned to Europe.

Another reception was tendered him at the Comite Franco-Amerique, where he again met Marshals Joffre and Lyautey, and Gabriel Hanotaux, president of the Comite. In an emotional address, Garbiel Hanotaux said, "When we think of the *Spirit of St. Louis* we think of Lafayette and Washington, and we think of Lindbergh." His response to the Comite concluded with the words, "I shall never forget Paris. We [meaning the plane and himself] had no intention of going home so soon, but cables from America make my return imperative." Roars of "Vive Lindbergh" followed his brief speech.

CHAPTER XVIII

The Ambassador of the Air Leaves for Home

THE cruiser *Memphis*, which President Coolidge had sent to France to take back to America the youth who in two short weeks had accomplished what diplomats and official cabinets had failed to effect, a happy accord with foreign nations, arrived at Cherbourg at seven o'clock on Friday night. The destroyer *Breck*, which was first chosen as the ship to carry him home, was also in the harbor, to participate in the farewell ceremonies.

It was the first time that a cruiser had ever been placed at the services of a private individual. In emergencies, both American and foreign diplomats have been carried, and refugees from wars and disasters have been taken aboard, but it was the first time a United States warship had changed its sailing date for the accommodation of a non-official guest.

The *Spirit of St. Louis* had been picked up by the *Memphis* at Southampton. Patiently it lay in two wooden cases, the weight of both approximately three tons.

Meanwhile, Captain Lindbergh was spending his last night in the city which had welcomed him as a beloved son. Frankly tired from his arduous duties, and acknowledging that sleep was a thing he looked most longingly toward, the airman returned to the Embassy after a short visit of farewell to the Paris

Post of the American Legion, to try to get as much of the regulation eight hours of slumber as possible.

While a guest of the Legion, Captain Lindbergh spoke briefly. "I had hoped to remain over long enough to see the Legion convention in Paris," he said, "even though I am too young to have been a member."

"You are a member," came a cry from all corners, making his election unanimous.

All day long the front door bell of the Embassy had been rung steadily by those eager to offer gifts for the American flier. One of the most attractive was the gold medal of the city of Paris, which had been struck since Lindbergh visited the Hôtel de Ville. It was presented, in person, by the president of the Municipal Council.

Promptly at six o'clock Saturday morning the aviator was out of bed and making ready for those last hours before he left for Cherbourg. He dined with Ambassador Herrick and his family at seven-thirty, a hearty American breakfast which showed as plainly as anything that excitement and nerves, which upset the strongest of men, are unknown to the healthy youth.

Ambassador Herrick declared that his guest had brought to the Embassy the good old-fashioned breakfast.

"Through all these years that I have been here, I have become accustomed to French breakfasts of coffee and rolls, but when the boy arrived I knew he must have real hearty morning provender. It almost demoralized the French chef, but the servants did their darnedest, scouring the neighborhood for ham and sausages and cereal and grapefruit. I don't think the boy missed anything—except pie."

At 8.30 Captain Lindbergh, accompanied by Ambassador Herrick and his son, Parmalee Herrick, arrived at Le Bourget field. On Friday, at a formal meeting of French army aviators at Le Bourget, all seeking and eager to escort the young airman from Paris to Cherbourg, where he had first crossed into France, Adjutant Herrisse and Sergeant Charpentier were the lucky ones awarded the honor. The adjutant was selected, also, to bring back the army combat plane in which the American aviator made the trip.

At the field, everything was in readiness for the flight to the coast. There, too, the youthful flier found Costes and Rignot preparing to try to beat the nonstop record which had been Lindbergh's since he landed in France. He declared he was honored at being able to see them off, and wished them Godspeed.

At one side of the field stood a new Breguet No. 19, one of the most modern types of French military machines, which had been loaned to Captain Lindbergh for his flight to Cherbourg. Accompanied by officials and officers, he went immediately to inspect it. For five minutes he listened intently to the French aviators who told him how to work the controls.

There was little formal leaving, when the time came for Captain Lindbergh to depart. Every plane belonging to the Thirty-fourth Regiment of aviation was drawn up in parade in his honor, but aside from this glistening array, there was no conventional demonstration. The very quiet which settled upon the big field was a compliment in itself, as though those who were there had hearts filled with emotion too deep for utterance.

Ambassador Herrick put his arm about the tall, slender boy, who had become almost like a son to him, and with his sentiments plainly upon his face said *au revoir* and wished him good luck. Captain Lindbergh also was affected by the poignant last few moments in Paris, and faltered as he thanked his host for the many kindnesses extended to him.

"When you come to America," he said, "I want you to come to see me."

After shaking hands with those nearest to him, he hurried to the plane and, although handling a strange machine, made a perfect take-off.

The streets were thronged with people eager to get a last glimpse of the "Lone Eagle" who had flown into their hearts such a short time before. But, although their shouts flew toward the flier and his escort, the sound was muffled as though they too were too emotional to give full vent to their farewell.

At Lessay, where Captain Lindbergh landed on the last lap of his flight to Cherbourg, he received an ovation. The forty-mile highroad leading from the field to Cherbourg was filled since early morning with people anxious to see the American hero. Every window was filled with flowers and eager faces, and American flags waved from the houses. The crowd was kept well in hand by the police and the marines.

After Lindbergh had made a perfect landing, the official reception committee approached him, and after a speech was delivered by the Mayor of Lessay, luncheon was served. Champagne was the pièce de résistance, but, following his usual custom, the young airman merely touched his lips to the glass when he was toasted. After a short speech, he proceeded to sign his name for all who asked for his autograph.

A pleasant message awaited him at the *Memphis*, when Commander David W. Bagley announced that a cablegram had been received from President Coolidge inviting Lindbergh and his mother to be guests at the temporary White House in Dupont Circle for a few days.

Everything had been done on the *Memphis* to make the intrepid airman as comfortable as possible, in spite of the fact that it is a man-of-war and unaccustomed to private individuals.

"This ship may not be one of those floating palaces," said an officer, "but, by George, it's roomier than the one he came over on." Commander Bagley had turned over to Lindbergh a three-room suite. The cabin in which Lindbergh slept was about eight by fourteen feet, with one window. The table, chairs, and desk were neat but comfortable. There was a smaller room adjoining and a tiled bath.

Admiral Burrage greeted the young flier on the quay in the name of the American Nation, and escorted him to the *Memphis*. The destroyer *Breck* lay close at hand, and with the bluejackets on the *Memphis*, gave three cheers as Captain Lindbergh went on board, while the band played the national anthem.

One of the first things the flier asked when he stepped aboard was if his "ship" was all right.

"Fine!" he said when assured it was snugly stored away. "I want it to be right near me."

CHAPTER XIX

The Blood and Faith of Lindbergh and His Ancestors

WHEN Lindbergh landed in Le Bourget, everybody at the same moment wanted to know all about him, his people, the blood that animated him, his appearance, his religious faith, in a word, the spirit and substance of the man.

It was not enough that he, a greatly daring unit of humanity, should lift the soul of man to the highest pinnacle of daring in that lone flight of his above the earth where mankind has been bound by its fears and lack of aërial knowledge ever since the dawn of creation. It was not enough to know that he was a tall, lean, strong youth of twenty-five with a shy, crooked smile that transformed a tanned, high-cheeked countenance as sunlight transforms a waterfall into jeweled radiance, that he had never used tobacco or alcohol in any form and only occasionally drank coffee. Everybody wanted to know the details that mark man from man.

Charles Augustus Lindbergh, as his entire name indicates, is, on his father's side, of unmixed Swedish blood. That paternal half also colored his formative years with occasional attendance at the Bethel Lutheran Church of Little Falls, Minn. During his father's life, the youth and the man were constant and understanding companions.

Upon his mother's side the blood is Irish,

9

English, and French. Lodge, Land, and Kissane are the names that stand out in the ancestral history. "I am proud that one of my mother's ancestors was French," said the flier in one of his direct and always tactful speeches in Paris. "It helps me to understand everybody here."

The flier was born in Detroit, February 4, 1902, at 1220 Forest Avenue West. Charles A. Lindbergh, an attorney at Little Falls, Minn., and Mrs. Evangeline Land Lindbergh, of Detroit, were his parents. His paternal grandfather, who came to America in 1860, was Augustus Lindbergh. He was born in Stockholm and served in the Swedish Parliament before coming to the United States, with his son, the father of Captain Lindbergh, then a baby of one year.

THE FOREBEARS OF THE ACE OF THE ATLANTIC

That sturdy grandfather foreshadowed the career of his hero grandson by his own individuality and stoical nerve. An unlucky misstep one day threw him into a buzz saw and amputation of an arm was the consequence. His calm acceptance of the accident was, at the time, a lesson in true manhood to his whole community.

The father of Captain Lindbergh was brought up near Melrose, Minn. He spent most of his boyhood hunting and fishing because there was no regular school in that part of the country. He was instructed carefully by the rugged former parliamentarian, his father. In 1881, at the age of twenty-one, he entered Grove Lake Academy, and in 1887 graduated from the University of Michigan with the degree of Bachelor of Laws. He then went back to Minnesota and practiced law.

As a lawyer, his friends state, he picked cases not by the size of the fee he hoped to get, but by merit, and if he believed in his client's case, he fought it through, even though, many times, he paid the expenses out of his own pocket. The result was, that in the anti-trust movement of 1906, he was elected to Congress from the Sixth Minnesota district. He was a candidate for Governor on the Farmer-Labor ticket when death came to him.

The mother of the flier whose clear, candid character so greatly formed his own is the daughter of Dr. C. H. Land, whose father was born in Hamilton, Ontario, and whose grandfather, Colonel John Land, is generally credited with being the founder of Hamilton. Colonel Land was born in England, probably in Suffolk, according to John C. Lodge, acting Mayor of Detroit, uncle of Mrs. Evangeline Lindbergh.

Mrs. Lindbergh's mother, who was Evangeline Lodge, was born in New York City, 1850, the daughter of Dr. Edwin A. Lodge, a homeopathic physician, son of George Lodge, a barrister. The ancestry of George Lodge goes back to Norman times. Evangeline Land's mother was Emma Kissane, who came with the first Irish influx to the county of Kent, Ontario.

COMRADESHIP OF MOTHER AND SON

Close and understanding comradeship has always existed between this mother and son. It was a thrill equally as great as his feather-light landing in Le Bourget that came to him when in the American

Embassy a few hours after that landing he heard her voice from Detroit over the newly installed transatlantic phone exhorting him to "be sure to get enough rest." She knew how tense aviators become after long flights and how deeply and completely they must relax, for she had flown with him a number of times and knew him to the innermost recesses of his brave heart.

To her, he is the dearest thing on earth, her shy and greatly daring son. To those who search for the roots of action in blood heritages, he is half Swedish and for the rest of him, English, Irish, French, and perhaps traces of other strains. For most of the world, he is that new blend and breed, an American.

For posterity, he will be as he is today to his friends, ALL MAN.

THE MOTHER'S IRISH LINEAGE

The mother of the Lone Eagle is the authority for the statement that Irish blood had its share in the making of her hero son. Two ancient Irish families, the Kissanes and the Healys, are named by her as contributing to his manhood.

A letter to Mrs. Lindbergh from John J. Murphy, president of the American Irish Historical Society, evoked this information. Following is the correspondence:

"*Mrs. Evangeline L. Lindbergh,*
Cass Chemical High School,
Detroit, Mich.

"DEAR MADAM:

"On behalf of the American Irish Historical Society, I beg to tender you our heartiest congratulations on the amazing achievement of your splendid son and his brilliant triumph over the perils of his undertaking. To you we offer our grateful thanks for calling the world's attention to his Irish inheritance.

"The American Irish Historical Society exists for the purpose of recording the deeds of men of Irish birth and descent in America. I would take it as a great favor, if, when you can spare the time, you would let us have the record of your mother's maiden name, the time of her arrival in the United States and the place of residence of her family in Ireland, and any other details which may be available. This information will be put in durable form and preserved in the archives of the society, which has a fireproof vault especially constructed for the purpose of preserving such material indefinitely.

"In the hope that you will accede to my request, I am,

"Sincerely yours,
"JOHN J. MURPHY."

Mrs. Lindbergh's reply was as follows:
"DEAR SIR:
"According to my grandfather's records, my mother's mother, Emma B. Kissane, was born December 10, 1818, in Douglas, Isle of Man, where the family moved from Tipperary. They later returned to Ireland. Her mother and father were William and Aphra Kissane. (I believe that Aphra Kissane was a Healy.)

"My mother, Evangeline Lodge (daughter of Edwin A. Lodge, born in London, England), was born in Broome Street, New York City, in 1850.

"My grandmother's brother, Reuben Kissane, took the name of Lloyd and is well known in the records and history of the City of San Francisco.

"Do not thank me for revealing Irish inheritance— all Irish descendants boast of it.

"EVANGELINE L. LINDBERGH."

CHAPTER XX

CARRYING THE AIR MAIL

SHORTLY before he flew off into the unknown from Roosevelt Field, New York, Lindbergh was covering the St. Louis-to-Chicago air-mail route for the Robertson Aircraft Corporation of Anglum, Missouri. It was while beating his lonely way by day and night over familiar air lanes that the twenty-five-year-old youth conceived the idea of the New York to Paris flight. And it was the spirit of the United States air-mail service that carried him over the ocean in the face of fearful odds.

LINDBERGH'S "APPOINTED ROUND"

Over the façade of the General Post Office Building, on Eighth Avenue, New York, is the inscription: "Neither snow nor rain nor heat nor gloom of night stays these couriers from the swift completion of their appointed rounds." That was the spirit of Lindbergh. His "appointed round" was New York to Paris for the time being, and nothing stayed him from its swift completion.

Many risks must be taken by air-mail pilots, and it is a tribute to the service that it has developed fliers of the type of Lindbergh—fine, clean, quick-thinking, highly skilled young fellows who fear neither fog nor night, nor storm nor tempest.

"Those men don't get credit for it," said Lindbergh at the moment of his triumph in Paris. His mind was running back to the men of the air-mail service, in whose company he really learned the flying game. "It" meant going through sleet and rain and fog to get the job done and make schedule. It is worth while setting down here the fact that the United States air-mail fliers carried on so well that the 1926 record shows 1,860,190 miles flown out of 1,987,834 scheduled— almost as close to 100 per cent performance as any service can show.

On his flight across the Atlantic, when Lindbergh ran into a sleet storm he detoured; he flew low until he almost skimmed the surface of the waves; he climbed to ten thousand feet. But he kept on and outflew the storm. That was the air-mail-service habit. It has been suggested that a possible explanation of the misfortune which befell Nungesser and Coli was that sleet was a hazard which their experience had not fitted them to cope with.

There is this to be said, however: the pilots of the air mail follow certain specified routes, and they become accustomed to these routes. Lindbergh stepped off alone on a cross-Atlantic venture where for hundreds of miles he had not a landmark to guide him.

Lindbergh began his aërial career at nineteen, leaving his home in Little Falls, Minn., where his father was a lawyer and member of Congress, and going to Lincoln, Nebraska, for his first lessons. Later he bought his own plane, and when he was appointed a flying cadet in the army, flew his aircraft to Kelly Field, San Antonio, Texas. He is now a colonel and flight commander in the 110th Observation Squadron, Missouri National Guard air unit in St. Louis.

For a year after leaving the army he flew in various independent enterprises, including several flying circuses. Finally he was appointed chief pilot on the St. Louis-Chicago air-mail route, from which he was given an indefinite leave of absence to prepare for his Atlantic Ocean hop.

In his congratulatory message to Mrs. Evangeline Land Lindbergh, mother of Colonel Lindbergh, Postmaster General New said:

"I offer the congratulations of the Post Office Department on your son's marvelous accomplishment. You have a boy to be proud of. We are proud of him too. He has contributed the most notable chapter in the history of aviation."

"ADOPTED" BY THE POSTAL SERVICE

Although Lindbergh served as an air-mail pilot for little more than a year, he has been adopted by the entire postal service as its own, the Postmaster General said, adding that he is a typical representative of the air-mail fliers whose united efforts reel off 15,752 air miles daily in transporting the mails.

"What we like most about Lindbergh," the Postmaster General said, "is his modesty and the straightforward business-like way in which he prepared for his epoch-making flight without the blaring of horns or the pursuit of personal publicity. Such publicity as he received has been attracted naturally by what he has actually done.

"It is a marvelous accomplishment. In fact, we scarcely realize how wonderful it all is. It is remarkable from whatever standpoint considered. First, the indomitable nerve and courage of the man who undertook it; next his accomplishment as a navigator and again the marvel from the standpoint of mechanics that a machine could be made to accomplish such a wonderful flight.

"It is a matter of special pride to the Post Office Department that one of the pilots of the air mail has set this standard for all aviators to shoot at. You can't beat those boys anywhere in any service in the world."

THE FIRST AIR-MAIL ROUTE

It was on May 15, 1918, that the first air-mail route in the United States was established between Washington, D. C., and New York City. It was at first inaugurated in conjunction with the War Department, which furnished planes and personnel and handled flying and maintenance operations, the Post Office Department taking care of the mail and matters pertaining thereto. In August of the same year the Post Office Department took over the entire operation of the route, and continued it until 1921.

Meantime the Department had been working toward the establishment of a transcontinental service. The first leg was established between Cleveland and Chicago in May, 1919; the second leg, New York to Cleveland, in July, 1919; the third leg, Chicago to Omaha, in May, 1920; and the last leg, Omaha to San Francisco, in September, 1920.

FLYING BY NIGHT

It was in 1923 that the Post Office Department decided to carry out certain experiments to determine whether cross-country night flying on regular schedule was feasible. Up to that year very little night flying had been done. Some experiments had been carried on, and the necessary equipment had been developed, but there had been very little cross-country flying at night on regular schedule.

Beacon lights were installed between Chicago and Cheyenne; airplanes were equipped with landing lights; emergency fields were prepared and marked, and terminal fields lighted. Pilots were given an opportunity to make practice night flights.

A regular schedule was fixed between New York and San Francisco in August, 1923, the portion of the route between Chicago and Cheyenne being flown at night. Begun experimentally, the service proved a complete success eventually.

The regular transcontinental service went into effect in July, 1924, and has been operating continuously since then with only slight changes in schedule, and with a performance percentage of approximately ninety-four per cent. Numerous changes in the lighted airway, looking toward a more efficient and economical administration, have been made, and additional lights have been installed, providing a powerful rotating beacon at approximately every fifteen miles.

CONTRACT ROUTES

In the development of the air-mail service a forward step was taken when the Postmaster General was authorized by law to enter into contracts for the transportation of mail by aircraft. This led to the establishment of several contract lines early in 1926. Since then numerous contract routes have been put in operation; most of these make direct connection with the government-operated transcontinental or New York-Chicago overnight service, delivering mail to and receiving mail therefrom.

Year in and year out, in fair weather and in bad, and over mountains and over plains, the Air Mail carries the mail from coast to coast, and over a number of lines connecting with the transcontinental route. No service in the world has abler or more versatile airmen. No training school for record-making achievements could be finer, for the Air Mail does not wait for fine weather. Rarely is it necessary to suspend a scheduled flight, the number of postponements during the year being very small. This has only occurred when a storm or fog blankets the whole region.

The transportation of mail, day after day, in winter and summer, between the Goddess of Liberty and the Golden Gate, may be said to mark the first real development of aviation in the United States.

Lindbergh is a remarkable product of that development, and his flight from New York to Paris in thirty-three and a half hours has led hopeful writers to predict that an air mail between America and Europe will be in operation before many years have passed.

CHAPTER XXI

LINDBERGH, LEAPER FROM THE CLOUDS

THE flier was chatting in his easy, informal manner with French and American newspaper men in the home of Ambassador Herrick two days after his dramatic arrival in Paris.

"Don't you resent being called the 'Flying Fool'?" queried one of the Americans.

Lindbergh's brows lowered over his light blue eyes. His mouth straightened in a thin, hard line.

"I certainly do resent it," he said, and his voice for the first time since he left New York showed annoyance and a trace of indignation. "I take no foolish risks and study out everything I do in the air. I don't think I am a flying fool."

His momentary indignation was based on good reason. From the beginning of his flying career he took chances only after he had looked on both sides and all around the particular exploit he was about to undertake. He knew by keen observation the way planes twist in the air and fall when out of control, how to right and bring back to a level keel a dead ship before crawling out on a wing and trusting one's life to a parachute.

He learned how to dive from a doomed plane so that the lines of the parachute might not be fouled, how to care for the rip cord and how to use flares and electric torch for forced night leaps and landings. No flier in the world has had greater experience in these hazards of the air and none has made such profitable use of this experience. Four times he has left ships at great heights to prepare coolly and with unshaken nerves for the ordeals of parachute leaps to safety. These have earned for him membership in the Caterpillar Club, composed of fliers who have made emergency leaps during flight and saved their lives thereby.

Lindbergh's fearless mastery of the air is written in the stories of these plunges from the clouds. In them one may read how completely the young man has sundered the fear cords that for uncounted ages have bound mankind to the earth, making them mere crawlers on the land and swimmers in some form or other over the waters.

Fortunately, the dauntless aviator has set down in accurate, characteristically brief reports exactly what happened to him and his ships in two of these emergencies. The first came on March 6, 1925, when he was a student aviator in the Army Flying School, Kelly Field, near San Antonio, Texas.

THE COLLISION IN THE AIR

He and Lieutenant C. D. McCallister were sent up to a height of 5000 feet for a practice attack upon a larger plane designated as the "enemy" flying at a lower level. How the two attacking planes collided in the dive and became locked in midair and how the two youngsters made their jumps is told in Lindbergh's official report as follows:

"A nine-ship SE-5 formation, commanded by Lieutenant Blackburn, was attacking a De Haviland 4-B, flown by Lieutenant Russell Maughan (dawn to dusk pilot), at about 5000-foot altitude and several hundred feet above the clouds. I was flying on the left of the top unit, Lieutenant McCallister on my right, and Cadet Love leading. When we nosed down on the DH, I attacked from the left and Lieutenant McCallister from the right. After Cadet Love pulled up I continued to dive on the DH for a short time before pulling up to the left. I saw no other ship near by.

"I passed above the DH and a moment later felt a slight jolt, followed by a crash. My head was thrown forward against the cowling and my plane seemed to turn around and hang nearly motionless for an instant. I closed the throttle and saw an SE-5 with Lieutenant McCallister in the cockpit a few feet away on my left. He was apparently unhurt and getting ready to jump.

"Our ships were locked together with the fuselage approximately parallel. My right wing was damaged and was folded back slightly, covering the forward right-hand corner of the cockpit. Then the ships started to mill around and the wires began whistling. The right wing commenced vibrating and striking my head at the bottom of each oscillation. I removed the rubber band safetying the belt, unbuckled it, climbed out past the trailing edge of the damaged wing, and with my feet on the cowling on the right side of the cockpit, which was then in a nearly vertical position, I jumped backward as far from the ship as possible.

"I had no difficulty in operating the pull ring and experienced no sensation of falling. The wreckage was falling nearly straight down and for some time I fell in line with its path.   Fearing the wreckage might fall on me, I did not pull the rip cord until I had dropped several hundred feet and into the clouds.

FALLING THROUGH THE CLOUDS

"During this time I had turned one-half revolution and was falling flat and face downward.   The parachute functioned perfectly; almost as soon as I pulled the rip cord and the risers jerked on my shoulders, the leg straps tightened, my head went down, and the chute was fully opened.

"I saw Lieutenant McCallister floating above me and the wrecked ships pass about one hundred yards to one side, continuing to spin to the right and leaving a trail of lighter fragments along their path.   I watched them until, still locked together, they crashed in the mesquite about two thousand feet below and burst into flames several seconds after impact.

"Next I turned my attention to locating a landing place.   I was over mesquite and drifting in the general direction of a plowed field, which I reached by slipping the chute.   Shortly before striking the ground, I was drifting backward, but was able to swing around in the harness just as I landed on the side of a ditch less than a hundred feet from the edge of the mesquite.

"Although the impact of the landing was too great for me to remain standing, I was not injured.   The parachute was still held open by the wind and did not collapse until I pulled on one group of the shroud lines.

"During my descent I lost my goggles, a vest pocket camera, which fitted tightly in my hip pocket, and the rip cord of the parachute."

A LEAP THROUGH THE SNOWSTORM

The second official report tells of his leap at night through a blinding snow and rain storm that blotted out all sight of the earth. This was made November 3, 1925.

"I took off from Lambert-St. Louis Field at 4.20 P. M., November 3," he wrote the Chief of the Air Mail Service, "arrived at Springfield, Ill., at 5.15, and, after a five-minute stop for mail, took the air again and headed for Peoria.

"The ceiling at Springfield was about 500 feet, and the weather report from Peoria, which was telephoned to St. Louis earlier in the afternoon, gave the flying conditions as entirely passable.

"I encountered darkness about 25 miles north of Springfield. The ceiling had lowered to around 400 feet and a light snow was falling. At South Pekin the forward visibility of ground lights from a 150-foot altitude was less than one-half mile and over Pekin the town lights were indistinct from 200 feet above. After passing Pekin I flew at an altimeter reading of 600 feet for about five minutes, when the lightness of the haze below indicated that I was over Peoria. Twice I could see lights on the ground and descended to less than 200 feet before they disappeared from view. I tried to bank around one group of lights, but was unable to turn quickly enough to keep them in sight.

"After circling in the vicinity of Peoria for thirty minutes I decided to try to find better weather conditions by flying northeast toward Chicago. I had ferried a ship from Chicago to St. Louis in the early afternoon and at that time the ceiling and visibility

10

were much better near Chicago than elsewhere along the route.

SEEKING A NIGHT LANDING

"Enough gasoline for about one hour and ten minutes' flying remained in the main tank and twenty minutes' in the reserve. This was hardly enough to return to St. Louis, even had I been able to navigate directly to the field by dead reckoning and flying blind the greater portion of the way. The only lights along our route at present are on the field at Peoria; consequently, unless I could pick up a beacon on the transcontinental route my only alternative would be to drop the parachute flare and land by its light, together with what little assistance the wing lights would be in the snow and rain. The territory toward Chicago was much more favorable for a night landing than that around St. Louis.

"I flew northeast at about 2000 feet for thirty minutes, then dropped down to 600 feet. There were numerous breaks in the clouds this time and occasionally ground lights could be seen from over 500 feet. I passed over the lights of a small town and a few minutes later came to a fairly clear place in the clouds.

DROPPING LIKE A ROCK

"I pulled up to about 600 feet, released the parachute flare, whipped the ship around to get into the wind and under the flare which lit at once, but instead of floating down slowly, dropped like a rock. For an instant I saw the ground, then total darkness. My ship was in a steep bank and for a few seconds after being blinded by the intense light I had trouble righting it.   I then tried to find the ground with the wing lights, but their glare was worse than useless in the haze.

"When about ten minutes' gas remained in the pressure tank, and still I could not see the faintest outline of any object on the ground, I decided to leave the ship rather than attempt to land blindly.   I turned back southwest toward less populated country and started climbing in an attempt to get over the clouds before jumping.

The main tank went dry at 7.51, and the reserve at 8.10.   The altimeter then registered approximately 14,000 feet, yet the top of the clouds was apparently several thousand feet higher.   I rolled the stabilizer, cut the switches, pulled the ship up into a stall, and was about to go out over the right side of the cockpit when the right wing began to drop.   In this position the plane would gather speed and spiral to the right, possibly striking my parachute after its first turn.

DIVING OVER THE SIDE

"I returned to the controls, and after righting the plane dived over the left side of the cockpit while the airspeed registered about seventy miles per hour and the altimeter 13,000 feet.

"I pulled the rip cord immediately after clearing the stabilizer.   The Irving chute functioned perfectly.   I had left the ship head first and was falling in this position when the risers whipped me around into an upright position and the chute opened.

"The last I saw or heard of the DH was as it disappeared into the clouds just after my chute opened. I placed the rip cord in my pocket and took out my flash light. It was snowing and very cold. For the first minute or so the parachute descended smoothly, then commenced an excessive oscillation which continued for about five minutes and which I was unable to check.

LANDING ON A BARBED WIRE FENCE

"The first indication that I was near the ground was a gradual darkening of the space below. The snow had turned to rain and although my chute was thoroughly soaked its oscillation had greatly decreased. I directed the beam from the 500-foot spotlight downward, but the ground appeared so suddenly that I landed directly on top of a barbed wire fence without seeing it.

"The fence helped to break my fall and the barbs did not penetrate the heavy flying suit. The chute was blown over the fence and was held open for some time by the gusts of wind before collapsing. I rolled it up into its pack and started toward the nearest light. Soon I came to a road which I followed about a mile to the town of Covell, Ill., where I telephoned a report to St. Louis and endeavored to obtain some news of where the ship had landed. The only information that I could obtain was from one of a group of farmers in the general store, a Mr. Thompson, who stated that his neighbor had heard the plane crash, but could only guess at its general direction.

"I rode with Mr. Thompson to his farm and after leaving the parachute in his house we canvassed the neighbors for any information concerning the plane. After searching for over an hour without result I left instructions to place a guard over the mail in case it was found before I returned and went to Chicago for another ship.

THE WRECKED PLANE

"On arriving over Covell the next morning I found the wreck with a small crowd gathered about it less than 500 feet back of the house where I had left the parachute. The nose and wheels had struck the ground at about the same time and after sliding along for about 75 feet it had piled up in the pasture beside a hedge fence. One wheel had come off and was standing inflated against the wall of the inside of a hog house a hundred yards farther on. It had gone through two fences and the wall of the house. The wings were badly splintered, but the tubular fuselage, although badly bent in places, had held its general form even in the mailpit. The parachute from the flare was hanging on the tailskid.

"There were three sacks of mail in the plane. One, a full bag, from St. Louis, had been split open and some of the mail was oil soaked but legible. The other two were only partially full and were undamaged.

"I delivered the mail to Maywood by plane to be dispatched on the next ships out."

A PLUNGE THROUGH A FOG BANK

On a later occasion he saved his life by a plunge in a parachute through a fog bank. It was when he was flying with mail from St. Louis to Chicago. He had piloted his plane as far as Marseilles and the Illinois River, and there the fog extended from the ground up to about six hundred feet, and as he was unable to fly under it he turned back and attempted to drop a flare and land. The flare did not function, and he again headed for Chicago. The story of what happened is best given in his own report:

"The fog extended from the ground up to about six hundred feet, and as I was unable to fly under it, I turned back and attempted to drop a flare and land. The flare did not function and I again headed for Maywood, hoping to find a break in the fog over the field there.

"I continued on a compass course of fifty degrees until 7.15 o'clock when I saw a dull glow on the top of the fog. This indicated a town below. There were several of these light patches on the fog, visible only when looking away from the moon, and I knew them to be towns bordering Maywood."

Maywood is Chicago's air-mail port. Lindbergh was not able to locate it. "Several times," he says, "I descended to the top of the fog, which was eight hundred to nine hundred feet high, according to my altimeter. The sky above was clear with the exception of scattered clouds, and the moon and stars were brightly shining.

"After circling around for thirty-five minutes, I headed west to be sure of clearing Lake Michigan, and in an attempt to pick up one of the lights on the transcontinental air course.

"Flying westward for fifteen minutes, and seeing no break I turned to the southwest hoping to strike the edge of the fog south of the Illinois river.   My engine quit at 8.28 o'clock and I cut in the reserve.   At that time I was up only 1500 feet and as the engine did not pick up as soon as I expected, I shoved the flash light in my belt and was about to release the parachute flare and jump, when the engine finally took hold again.   A second trial showed the main tank to be dry and, accordingly, a maximum of twenty minutes flying time left.

"There was not an opening anywhere in the fog and I decided to leave the ship as soon as the reserve tank was exhausted.   I tried to get the mail pit open with the idea of throwing out the mailsacks and then jumping, but I was unable to open the front buckle.   I knew that, with no gasoline in the tanks, the risk of fire was very slight, so I began to climb for altitude.   Then suddenly I saw a light on the ground for several seconds.

"This was the first light I had seen for nearly two hours, and as almost enough gasoline for fifteen minutes flying remained, I glided down to 1200 feet and pulled out the flare release cable as nearly as I could judge over the spot where the light had appeared.   This time the flare functioned, but it served only to illuminate the top of a solid bank of fog, into which it soon disappeared, without showing any trace of the ground.

"Seven minutes of gasoline remained in the gravity tank.   Seeing the glow of a town through the fog, I turned toward the open country and nosed the plane up.

STEPPING OUT INTO SPACE

"At 5000 feet the engine sputtered and died.   I stepped out on the cowling and out over the right side of the cockpit, pulling the rip cord after a hundred-foot fall.

"The parachute, an Irving seat service type, functioned perfectly. I was falling head downward when the risers jerked me into an upright position, and the chute opened. This time I saved the rip cord.

"I pulled the flash light from my belt and was playing it down toward the top of the fog when I heard the plane's engine pick up. When I jumped it had practically stopped dead, and I had neglected to cut the switches. Apparently when the ship nosed down, an additional supply of gasoline drained to the carburetor. Soon she came into sight about a quarter of a mile away headed in the general direction of my parachute.

"I put the flash light in a pocket of my flying suit, preparatory to slipping the parachute out of the way if necessary. The plane was making a left spiral of about a mile diameter and passed approximately three hundred yards away from my chute, leaving me on the outside of the circle.

"I was undecided as to whether the plane or I was descending the more rapidly, and I guided my chute away from the spiral path of the ship as rapidly as I could.

"The ship passed completely out of sight, but reappeared in a few seconds, its rate of descent being about the same as that of the parachute. I counted five spirals, each one a little farther away than the last, before reaching the top of the fog bank.

"When I settled into the fog I knew that the ground was within one thousand feet and reached for the flash light, but found it to be missing. I could see neither earth nor stars and had no idea what kind of territory was below. I crossed my legs to keep from straddling a branch or wire, guarded my face with my hands and waited.

"Presently I saw the outline of the ground and a moment later was down in a corn field.

"The corn was over my head and the chute was lying on top of the cornstalks. I hurriedly packed it and started down a corn row. The ground visibility was about one hundred yards. In a few minutes I came to a stubble field and some wagon tracks which I followed to a farmyard a quarter of a mile away.

"After reaching the farmyard I noticed automobile headlights playing over the roadside. Thinking that someone might have located the wreck of the plane, I walked over to the car. The occupants asked whether I had heard an airplane crash, and it required some time to explain to them that I had been piloting the plane and was searching for it myself. I had to display the parachute as evidence before they were thoroughly convinced."

CHAPTER XXII

In the Days of His Youth

LIKE many boys who developed genius in a particular line, Charles Lindbergh was an indifferent pupil at school. His mother acknowledges that it was difficult to interest him in branches which did not get his attention. He liked mathematics, but grammar and English did not appeal to him.

At school, those who knew and loved him, declared he was "a peculiar guy." Above all things he preferred to be alone. With no companion other than his dog he would spend entire days in the woods or pottering about the farm at Little Falls, Minnesota. He worked for weeks on a boat, and when it was finished launched it on one of the wood lakes, taking long, adventurous cruises with his dog as crew.

The father of the young American hero had nerves of steel and they supported him when he went through a serious abdominal operation without an anesthetic. During the operation he spent the time talking about the Federal Reserve system with a friend, who sat beside him.

There was deep sympathy between Charles and his father, and something stronger than the usual relationship between father and son developed between them. They were constantly together and spent hours in conversation. When his father died in 1924, Charles carried aloft the ashes of his beloved parent in his plane and scattered them over the family homestead and over the land which had been the background of their happiness.

He attended public school and went later to Little Falls High School, where he was graduated in 1918 at the age of sixteen. As a small boy he had a fondness for mechanics, and was always tinkering at things trying to find out "what made it go" and if there wasn't some way of making it "go faster."

THE INQUISITIVE MIND AT WORK

His experimental bent sometimes got him into hot water. Hazardous about himself, and many times doing stunts, which frightened his family, to find out the truth concerning equilibrium, he believed in submitting other things to hazard as well.

Cats had much cause for complaint, and one day the small daughter of a neighbor complained to Mrs. Lindbergh that Charles had been hurting her Angora kitten.

Mrs. Lindbergh immediately called Charles and questioned him.

"No, Mother, I didn't hurt the cat one bit," he said. His innocent blue eyes were turned up to her. His face was almost too beguiling, it seemed, to augur good for the cat. Mrs. Lindbergh persisted in her questioning.

"I really didn't hurt it, Mother," he replied again and again. "You see, somebody said if you dropped a cat, it didn't matter how far, it always fell on its feet. I pushed it off the porch, and when I looked down to see whether it had landed like that, it really did, right on its feet."

VARSITY DAYS

His interest in mechanics caused him to matriculate at the Univerity of Wisconsin in 1921, and he worked his way through a course in mechanical engineering.

His entire attention while at the University was given to his work. He put aside all outside pleasures, not that he was indifferent to friendships, but because his studies were infinitely more diverting. Far from being unsociable, he nevertheless stayed mostly by himself, using the time out of class and away from studies in experiments, going into this end of the work farther than was indicated by his curriculum. Nothing he undertook seemed too much trouble. He would apply himself doggedly for hours upon some device which withheld the secret of its mechanism, and refused to give it up until he had overcome the problem. This power of concentration became his greatest asset in the work of aviation which he was to take up later. The extraordinary fine balance of his mind in the matter of mechanical research, the infinite patience necessary to overcome the many irritating and difficult processes, were to be the means which led him up the steep road to success.

One of his main interests while at the university was the building of a curious contrivance which was a puzzle to all who saw it. The work was done under the back porch of the home of his closest friend, Delos Dudley, son of Professor and Mrs. W. H. Dudley of Madison.

It was an iceboat geared to an airplane propeller and run by a motor-cycle engine. Charles took great pride in it and sailed it on Lake Mendota in the winter of 1921. When it was wrecked in a collision with a real iceboat, he patched it up into working shape again and used it all winter.

Although he did not go in for athletics at college, he kept himself in excellent physical trim. Rigid self-discipline made him immune to ordinary physical fatigue.

"He would rather sleep on the floor than in bed," one of his friends declared. He was not a talker but a doer, and would pick out something extraordinary, which no one else would attempt, being sure beforehand that he could do it.

Social life did not appeal to him outside his small circle of staunch friends. He did not care for dancing or girls, and was usually in bed early. Smoking and drinking never attracted him and he abstained from both. Long tramps, with his toothbrush and other few needs tucked in his pocket, were all he needed for amusement. Later, when he became interested in aviation, he was a well-known figure in his big overalls, his goggles, helmet, and toothbrush in his pocket, ready to go off at a moment's notice.

THE FLYING INSTINCT

In 1921 he determined to become an aviator. He was nineteen when he left the university, and applied to the flying school at Lincoln for tuition. A big, ungainly figure, thoroughly rustic in appearance, he did not impress the instructors as having the usual qualifications for the work.   But a surprise was in store for them, as they discovered before many months. They had overlooked the keen eyes, the determined chin of the lad, and the calm serenity of his purposeful nature.   It soon developed that he had an uncanny aptitude for flying and an instinctive touch which comprises that rare thing in aviation, "air sense."

He learned the rudiments of flying, and his sixth sense doubled the value of what he had learned.   Parachute jumping was part of the curriculum, and this experience and his coolness were life-saving factors in days to come.

Although he had fulfilled every requirement in the school, he was not permitted to fly "solo."   This restriction annoyed him.   He had unlimited confidence in himself, and his one desire was to "go it alone." When he approached the instructors he was informed he must put up a $500 bond before he would be permitted to fly alone.   He did not have the money, and feeling such a demand was ridiculous, he left the flying school, and went on his own as a stunt flier.   In 1922 he went to Billings, Montana, flying and leaping to earth to advertise the garage of Robert Westover. He flew any plane offered and became known for the daring of his stunts.   While engaged in this hazardous means of making a living, he perfected his control of planes, and learned to make perfect feather-light landings.

HIS OWN PLANE

All the time he worked he was saving up every penny.   He did not indulge in any of the smaller weaknesses, for one idea was paramount, and that objective was a plane of his own. In March, 1923, the army was selling planes that it did not need. It was not a very alluring sale, but to one man who strolled about, looking keenly at the equipment and handling the machines, it was the greatest sale on earth. Charles Lindbergh went slowly about the jam of salvage, and finally selected a training plane. He inspected the motor and the controls, and poked about it until he was satisfied that this was the thing he had been looking for. It was a Curtiss "Jennie" and a good, sturdy machine.

On "Jennie" he lavished all the devotion he had formerly given to the boat in the woods, the iceboat, and his dog. He had it primed and in fine shape in a short time, and started off barnstorming on his own account. From country fair to country fair he flew, thrilling the countryside with his stunts, and taking a few of the more adventuresome for a flight.

During his travels about the country, he stopped at various flying fields in Michigan and in Texas and inspected the newest types of machines. They were very different from the ones in which he had served his apprenticeship. Every moment he could spare he spent among these planes, for these were the airships that he meant eventually to fly.

In March, 1924, a tall youth in a shabby, blue suit walked into the barracks of the Texas Flying School. It was Charles Lindbergh, an aspirant for army training. The lanky form caught the eyes of the other cadets, who looked at him with amusement.

"Going to be an aviator?" asked one.

"Been thinking about it," replied the boy indiffer-ently.

"Ever done any flying?"

"About 600 hours. I've been barnstorming for some time. Flew down here."

"Where's your plane?" was the abrupt and suspicious question.

"Landed at Stinson Field. Will trot it over to-morrow."

The next day the band of skeptical students gathered about a plane, which appeared to have been in a terrific battle and had come out much worse for wear. The fabric was torn off in great pieces from one wing.

"Why do you fly without fabric?" was asked.

"It costs money. I can fly without it, if I want to, can't I?"

And to show the truth of his words, he hopped into the plane and showed that it was not only probable but possible.

The youngster with such nonchalant courage appealed to the men, and he immediately became a favorite. They would have liked to "get his goat" but they found that they could not do it. If tricks were to be played, he, too, was good at the game.

While he joined in the pranks of the cadets to a certain extent, his main interest was the routine of the school. Its standard is the highest of its kind and he rose determinedly to meet it. It was impossible to get him into a poker game, a drinking bout, or to call upon a girl. He kept his mind and body as finely keyed for the difficult work as a racing airplane which stands ready to be off at a moment's notice.

THE FLYING SCHOOL AT KELLY FIELD

The six months' course was rigid, and barely one-fourth of his classmates were advanced. Lindbergh passed the many tests, and in his ground subjects attained an average of 93 per cent. He was sent up to the advanced flying school at Kelly Field and placed under Lieutenant Thomas W. Blackburn.

"Just one of those lanky boys who stand around and do what you tell them," recalled Lieutenant Blackburn. "He did creditable work at Kelly Field but did not distinguish himself."

But, though Lindbergh did not make a deep impression upon the instructors, he was considered by his classmates as the best pilot in the class. At the end of the year he won a commission in the reserve corps. At graduation every man but the one who was destined to become a world hero, wore the uniform to which he was entitled. When asked why he did not put it on, the boy said, "Don't want to attract attention."

The only kind of person Lindbergh cordially disliked was what is known as a "ground flier." He is the man who talks about what he is going to do but never does it. Lindbergh's contempt for the type was obvious, and this quality in some of the people he met was no doubt responsible for his own reticence. He never said what he meant to do. When he was ready to accomplish something, he did it. Those who knew him respected his silence, for they knew back of it was determination, and when the time come Lindbergh would "be there with the goods."

Determined now to make money which would enable him to become a really first-class flier, he went to work

11

for the Robertson Aircraft Corporation, and while there became an air-mail flier. His experience in parachute jumping was of immense value to him in this work, and several times saved his life. He escaped without injury on each occasion, but once was badly bruised when landing, and another time was in danger of being mangled by the wild gyrations of his unmanned plane as he drifted to earth. During his service as air-mail flier, he totaled 1800 hours in the air, which is equal to fifteen years' experience of the average aviator.

CHAPTER XXIII

The Lure of the Paris-New York Trophy

IT was in 1919, immediately after the flight of the *NC-4* to the Azores, Portugal, and England, that Raymond Orteig first offered an award of $25,000 for the aviators who accomplished a nonstop flight between New York and Paris. The award was limited to five years, and within this period there were no takers. The Atlantic was crossed by biplane from Newfoundland to Ireland; by dirigible from Scotland to America and back; and by hydroplane from Portugal to Brazil, but no one had attempted the New York-Paris flight.

In May, 1924, the Orteig award expired, but was promptly renewed for another five years. In that year, 1924, the round-the-world flight of the United States Army Air Service planes stimulated interest in aviation in general and the Orteig award in particular. Byrd's conquest of the pole by airplane, the flight of the Italian army plane from Rome to Australia and Japan and back, the flight of Sir Alan Cobham from London to Melbourne, and numerous other achievements served to whet the appetite for aviation exploits.

The first practical attempt to capture the trophy ended in disaster before the fliers left American soil. On September 21, 1926, the Sikorsky airplane in which Rene Fonck, famous French ace, and Lieut. L. W. Curtin, of the United States Navy, hoped to reach

Paris, was wrecked and burned when it tumbled into a twenty-foot gulley at the end of the starting runway at Roosevelt Field, N. Y.

There were two victims of that disaster—the mechanic, Jacob Islamoff, and the radio operator, Charles Clavier. But tragedy could not deter the bold spirits of the air.

Notwithstanding the peril by land and sea, fliers began to gather on Roosevelt Field, some of them internationally famous. Interest was centered there, but out of the West swept the unknown air-mail pilot, and, unaided, captured the coveted trophy and won fame in a day.

THE MAN WHO OFFERED THE $25,000 PRIZE

Raymond Orteig, who offered the award of $25,000 for the first nonstop flight by airplane between New York and Paris, is known as a French-American hotelman and the story of how he came to make his generous offer is worth telling.

During the war his hotels became headquarters for French officials who visited New York, and among these officials were army officers and aviators. There was much talk concerning the importance of the airplane, and Raymond Orteig became interested. When the Aëro Club of America banqueted Rickenbacker, he attended and grew so enthusiastic that he joined the club.

THREE SUCCESSFUL FLIGHTS

In 1919, three flights were made across the Atlantic, one by the seaplane *NC-4*, with a stop at the Azores;

one by a British biplane, a nonstop flight from Newfoundland to Ireland; and a round-trip flight, Scotland
to America and back, by a British dirigible.

The first of these, the flight of the *NC-4*, May 16–27,
aroused the enthusiasm of Orteig, but he expressed
regret that the famous plane completed the course to
London via the Azores and Portugal—with never a
stop in his beloved France.

He thought the thing over, and resolved to make it
worth while for aviators to make Paris the goal or the
starting point of a new record-making flight. On May
22, 1919, he approached the Aëro Club of America
with his offer of $25,000 for the first New York-Paris
flight. Following is his letter:

"Aëro Club of America,
297 Madison Avenue,
New York City.

"Gentlemen: As a stimulus to the courageous
aviators, I desire to offer through the auspices and
regulations of the Aëro Club of America a prize of
$25,000 to the first aviator of any allied country cross-
ing the Atlantic, in one flight, from Paris to New York
or New York to Paris, all other details in your care.
                "Yours very sincerely,
                        "RAYMOND ORTEIG."

The offer was accepted and a bank guaranty made.

On the morning after Lindbergh's arrival in Paris,
Raymond Orteig was one of the first to greet the young
winner of his $25,000 prize. He reached the French
capital after a special trip from the Pyrenees. "I feel

a lot lighter!" he exclaimed, and someone suggested, "about $25,000!"

"No," he replied, laughing. "I mean my spirits feel lighter at the thought of what this man has done."

Orteig is himself a man who has won fame from obscurity. Thirty years ago he was head waiter in the old New York Café Martin when it was on University Place. He was born in the French village of Louvre-Inzon and came to America in 1882. When the Café Martin moved farther uptown, Raymond Orteig became its owner. The place is now the Hotel Lafayette, and he also owns the Hotel Brevoort.

Known simply as Raymond to the patrons of the old Café Martin thirty years ago, and concerned only about pleasing his guests, M. Orteig is today very much a man of the world. He has made some sixty voyages across the Atlantic by water, and has hopes of crossing by air some day, now that Lindbergh has demonstrated that Paris and New York are only separated by less than a day and a half of flying.

CHAPTER XXIV

Ten Months of Preparation

THE dream that came true, came to Lindbergh in August of 1926. He was then chief pilot of the air-mail route between St. Louis and Chicago. His "air sense" was so remarkable that his fellow fliers unanimously acknowledged him as their chief. He knew all about engines, planes, and parachutes.

"That hop over the Atlantic isn't so much," he said repeatedly. "I can do it if I can get anybody to fix me up with a plane." •

One day he told this to Major William H. Robertson, head of the Aircraft Corporation that had the contract for the St. Louis-Chicago mail. His record for skill and courage was so extraordinary and his earnestness was such that Major Robertson believed him instantly.

"If anybody can jump the Atlantic and grab the Orteig prize," thought the Major, "Lindbergh can."

It was Major Robertson who made the first efforts to make the flier's dream come true. For months he talked about the project to moneyed men, but they smiled quizzically and passed on. It was early in 1927 when the Major spoke to Harry H. Knight, former flier and prominent in the financial world of St. Louis. On that day the plans for the flight really took shape. Mr. Knight and Major Robertson were soon joined by Major Albert Bond Lambert, pioneer of aviation in

St. Louis, for whom Lambert Flying Field is named, Harry H. Knight, Wooster Lambert, Harold N. Bixter, president of the St. Louis Chamber of Commerce, F. Lansing Ray, publisher of the St. Louis *Globe-Democrat*, Charles G. Richardson, and E. C. Thompson, all of St. Louis. Into the fund raised by these men Charles A. Lindbergh put $2000, his savings of years.

With this money at his back, Lindbergh demonstrated the stuff of which he is made by starting immediately to find a suitable plane for the record-breaking flight. He went first to New York to buy a Bellanca, but found that no delivery could be made on time. He then turned his attention to a Ryan monoplane, a ship he had always admired.

San Diego, where the Ryan Airlines plant turn out their beautiful and sturdy planes, was his next objective. There he found a kindred soul in Benjamin F. Mahoney, who believed at once in the intrepidity and ability of the tall, young mail flier who stood before him.

Within twenty-four hours of the time of that visit, draftsmen were at work upon the plans for the ship. The name had already been selected. The *Spirit of St. Louis* had been agreed upon by all who had contributed to the general fund.

From the first Lindbergh worked with the designers and later with the builders of the plane. He virtually lived in the Ryan plant, and every part of the ship has felt the touch of his hand.

For sixty days he worked and ate in the shop and as the long, graceful lines were formed under his eyes and hands, his quiet enthusiasm grew.

As the body of the ship matured, its soul was being prepared. Across the continent in the plant of the Wright Aëronautical Corporation in Paterson, N. J., a motor of the whirlwind type was being built. Aircooled and with nine cylinders of the radial type, it was planned to develop a maximum of 225 horsepower. When completed it looked like a stubby, nine-spoke wheel. Its tests upon the block in Paterson and later in San Diego proved it to be dependable. Its smooth, snoring whir was music to Lindbergh's ear, as it answered every call made upon it.

THE TRIAL FLIGHT OF THE "SPIRIT OF ST. LOUIS"

Then one day the beautiful body with its motor soul was wheeled from the hangar for its first flight. Lindbergh stepped into the specially designed cabin with its curious periscope attachment. His hand closed over the control, the engine was turned over, it commenced to whir, there was a short run, a light leap, and the *Spirit of St. Louis* was in its destined element.

When Lindbergh made his characteristically light landing, he was bubbling with praise of the ship. It was exactly what he wanted. With it he could cross the Atlantic, and, after refueling, hop back again if necessary. Indeed, he had no fear. It fitted him like his shoes.

THE HOP TO ST. LOUIS

No one outside of the backers of the project and a few of their intimates had known anything up to this time of Lindbergh's intentions. The first inkling came on May 10, when the *Spirit of St. Louis* was casually wheeled out upon its runway and Lindbergh nosed it up in the general direction of St. Louis.

Just as casually Lindbergh dropped down into Lambert Field next day. He had flown 1600 miles in 14 hours 25 minutes. His speeds ranged from 90 to 105 miles an hour. So true had been his reckoning that it came within fifteen miles of his objective. It was easy for him to make the necessary compass directions to get to the field before the time he had scheduled for himself.

In that record-breaking flight he had jumped over the Rockies and had passed over the perils of the desert without even a thought of danger.

Before he turned in for rest in St. Louis, he went all over the ship with the mechanics and was delighted to find that no defect appeared anywhere.

No weariness was in him as he jauntily seated himself for the hop from St. Louis to New York. This he made in 7 hours 20 minutes, a total of 21 hours and 45 minutes for a flight from the Pacific to the Atlantic. In that nonchalant two-hop journey many records were broken, but Lindbergh did not make note of them. He was too much occupied with the thought of what lay ahead.

LANDING IN NEW YORK

When he landed at Curtiss Field outside New York on May 12, the world began to take note of him. Here was one lone soul that proposed to make the flight that others were planning to make in groups of two or more. Here was a new plane that had never been put to a test of carrying a full load. "Surely," said the experts, "this brash young man will meet disaster."

These doubts somewhat faded when one talked to the tall, low-voiced, smiling young redhead. He seemed to take everything as part of the day's work. Patiently and methodically he checked up every bolt, screw, and strut of the *Spirit of St. Louis*. Again and again the whirlwind engine snored its whirring drone. He saw to the filtering of gasoline and lubricants. At the end of three days everything was ready. By the evening of May 15 he could have flown if the weather had been fair.

As the crowds thronged about him, besieging the hangars where Byrd worked over his *America* and Chamberlin tuned up his Bellanca, he watched the wind and the clouds. His mother came from Detroit to say good-by with a heroic love that would have put a Roman matron to shame. Still he watched the clouds. With him always was B. F. Mahoney, whose faith was one hundred per cent in the flier and one hundred per cent in the ship. With him also were the steadfast Harry H. Knight and his St. Louis associates, and they were all pulling for Lindbergh.

And then one night the wind came out of the west, the heavy clouds slowly lifted from the earth, and adventure beckoned to Lindbergh and the *Spirit of St. Louis*.

The dream he had dreamed was about to come true.

CHAPTER XXV

The New World Rejoices With the Old

BEFORE Lindbergh was an hour in the air the telephones to newspaper offices buzzed with anxious inquiries:

"Is Lindbergh still in the air?"

"How far out is he?"

"Why has he to go by way of Newfoundland?"

"Did he have a boat?"

"What ships is he likely to sight?"

"What land will he see first after he crosses the ocean?"

These and a thousand other inquiries kept the telephone wires of America busy. The bravery of the boy gripped and held the interest of the people as nothing had done since the final scene of the World War.

Eagerly the compatriots of Lindbergh, from coast to coast, read every scrap of news that had a bearing upon this gallant flight which had in it all the elements of a drama. They read of how the *Spirit of St. Louis*, with its lone pilot, had taken off from San Diego and had come roaring eastward, eating up the miles as if by magic; of how, straight as an arrow, Lindbergh had flown through the night, shut in his tiny compartment, guided only by his instruments and his instinctive genius for flying, and in the morning had found himself within fifteen miles of St. Louis.

They chuckled over the newspaper report that

although his earth-inductor compass had been thirty degrees off—the variations were bad in that part of the country—he had made St. Louis like a homing pigeon.

They read of how, when he reached St. Louis, he did not land at first, but zoomed up and circled over the city that people might see him—the only gesture unrelated to his flight which Lindbergh made on the way from the Pacific to Paris—and they told each other that it was the boy in him, unrestrained for the time being, expressing his joy over the way in which his plane had worked.

That was the note which touched all hearts—"the boy in him." It was the Boy spirit in all of us that made America seem delirious that Saturday when the news came that Lindbergh had been sighted over Ireland, on his way safely to the French capital. It explained a little of the great wave of feeling that rolled up around "the Boy's" exploits. As one writer said: "The emotions of a world, a little weary of fuddled politics, of messiness and jazz, were stirred. Its own lost daydreams have suddenly come to life in flesh and reality in a Boy Hero, who has cracked the thin veneer of its false sophistication."

LINDBERGH THE SOLE TOPIC

Small wonder that radio programs were interrupted to give the log of the flight, and that even the stolid train announcers in the big railroad stations broke in upon their "arrival and departure of trains on track so and so," to give the latest news of "Lucky" Lindbergh. Small wonder that business men were unable to fasten their minds on their own undertakings, and,

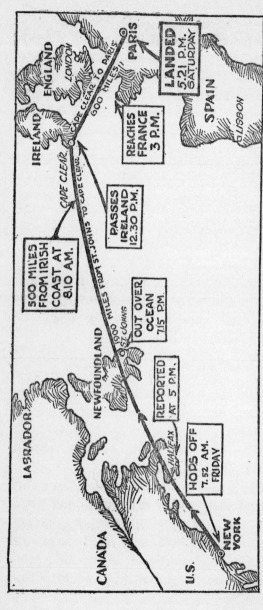

THE GREAT CIRCLE OVER WHICH LINDBERGH HOPPED

Almost without warning Lindbergh soared up from the western coast of America bound for Paris. He stopped only once on his transcontinental flight; that was at St. Louis. On Friday, May 20, at 7.52 in the morning he hopped off from New York and swung over the Great Circle of 3600 miles, landing at Le Bourget field, Paris, at 5.21 the following day. The chart indicates graphically the route taken by the young eagle. The actual calculated distance on the Great Circle between Mineola, L. I., latitude 40° 44′ 18″ N, longitude 73° 37′ W, and Paris, latitude 48° 50′ N, longitude 2° 20′ E, is 3135 nautical miles, which equals 3610.1 statute miles. The inductor compass which he carried enabled him to arrive over Ireland within three miles of his objective.

instead, discussed the details of the flight as communicated by the girls at the switchboards. Small wonder that crowds, growing in density each minute, collected around the bulletin boards of newspaper offices. Head and shoulders above every other news item, above every other topic of conversation, was the flight of this intrepid Jason of the wide Atlantic.

"Where is he now?"

"Oh, he is such a kid!"

"And all alone!"

"I bet he makes it!"

"He'll make it all right!"

Thus the chorus swelled. In every hamlet, every crossroads in the broad land, as well as in the great centers of population—indeed in every far-flung corner of the civilized world where the news of the day penetrates, humanity hung almost breathless upon the great adventure of Charles Lindbergh.

THE CONFIDENCE OF THE PEOPLE

There was a curious sort of confidence in the public mind regarding the outcome. Somehow America expected him to "make it." Not "Will he make it?" or "Can he make it?" was the burden of conversation and thought, but "He's going to make it!"

In that attitude of the public mind lies food for study by the psychologist. Why did this young man, barely twenty-five, flying with almost every conceivable handicap except bad weather, and taking his chances on that, have the confidence of a people who had been fearful for others better equipped and better known as flying men?

Let the answer come from the comments of people who gave no thought to psychology, but were able enough to phrase the feelings engendered in them by the stirring event.

"He's such a kid," said one man. "I don't know him—never saw him—but I know the type. I saw them in the war and I've seen them in business, and there's nothing can stop them. Half the time they seem to oldsters to be just blundering along without thought, but all at once the oldster wakes up to the fact that the kid has done something the older man in his wisdom would never have attempted."

A university professor turned to heredity for an explanation. "This young man," he said, "is only twenty-five, but there flows in his veins blood of the Vikings. One need only know his name to know that. His is the heritage of men who dared the sea when the sea was a place of mystery and terror to mankind; who fared forth over unknown waters to discovery and conquest."

Something nonchalant, almost insouciant, about the tall, slim Missouri National Guard officer had appealed to many persons. His two-hop flight from San Diego, where the plane was made, to New York, with a stop at St. Louis, where his flight was financed, brought him as an almost unheard-of stranger to the Eastern coast.

He was without publicity. He was almost as alone in his planning of the flight as he was in the cockpit of his plane when he took off for Paris. He sought no help. When it was offered, he grinned infectiously and gave thanks, but made no move of acceptance. When he was offered the use of a radio set which another aviator, tuning up as his rival, was not going to use, he only drawled, "Thanks. Maybe I might accept it some time."

A TRIBUTE TO HIS MOTHER

"I liked his attitude toward his mother and I liked her attitude toward him," was the way a gentle old lady summed up her feeling. "He is such a boy, and he looked so tall and strong, but so very, very young in the picture I saw of him standing by his mother. I liked the way she came all the way from Detroit, where she teaches school, to New York to see him before he started and then went back to her work without waiting for the start. I can understand that. She was afraid she might distract him at a critical time, but she was more afraid that she might yield to a mother's instinct at the last minute and be tempted to try to dissuade him from his quest for fame and fortune."

The very lack of organization which would have daunted most men served to endear the young air-mail flier to the popular mind. But the thing that most people dwelt upon was the fact that he went alone. They spoke of it with hushed voices. They tried to visualize what it meant:

No one to relieve him at the controls! No one to speak to! No one to consult if anything went wrong! Nothing but failure and death his sure fate if he lost consciousness for one moment of blessed sleep! No one to plot his course! No one to scan his dials for him! In front of his eyes only the high instrument board! No view of where he was headed but such as

12

he could get through a periscope, reaching its nose above the rim of the cockpit!

But the boy of the lion heart faced the desolation of the North Atlantic with high courage; and riding upon

the wings of his plane was probably the greatest cargo of good wishes ever carried by any venturer into the unknown.

"THE KID WINS!"

When the rumor of his arrival over Ireland was verified and he was reported nearing Paris the enthusiasm of America knew no bounds.

"Lindbergh! Lindbergh!" the name was on everyone's lips. People cheered and laughed and cried by turns. Staid gentlemen forgot their dignity and yelled with the abandon of the small boy. The banker and the bootblack met on common ground in their admiration for the young man who, out of clean living, sound idealism, and simple American faith, had wrought the greatest single-handed victory the world has seen.

Lindbergh traveled light. He made no talk about "gathering scientific data." He was just a boy who had set himself the job of flying to Paris—and "the kid won!" This was the cry shouted from the house-tops, displayed on the front pages of the newspapers, iterated and reiterated into the radio and telephone transmitters: "The kid wins!"

Around the bulletin boards the crowds danced and cheered. They wished Lindbergh back so that they might receive him with ovations, medals, palms, and chants of victory.

Oldsters recalled other great moments in their lives. Youngsters derided them and hotly contended that this was the finest, most heroic deed of all time! . . . And who could blame the youngsters? For here was a "Boy" for whom all the dreams of Boydom had come true. Out of the unknown he had come, obscure, unheralded—and he was destined to walk with kings!

CHAPTER XXVI

THE "SPIRIT OF ST. LOUIS"

IT is a matter for doubt if the sponsors of the first nonstop flight from New York to Paris named the good ship, which carried Charles Augustus Lindbergh to deathless fame, from anything but civic pride. Yet the first St. Louis, as King Louis the IX of France, was as bold an adventurer in his day as Lindbergh, and it may be that the name itself was a lucky omen of success.

Blind luck, however, had little to do with Lindbergh's exploit. Backed by years of experience with planes, motors, and instruments of every kind in the arduous service of the air mail, few men were better equipped to choose the best available equipment.

THE PLANE

There was little doubt in Lindbergh's mind as to the plane he wanted to use. On February 27 the Ryan Airlines received a telegram from him saying that he wanted a transatlantic plane. The company did about twenty-four hours' engineering work and when Lindbergh arrived the following day they were able to tell him that they could build the plane. At that time Lindbergh had never flown a Ryan plane, but ordered it entirely on its reputation and his own approval of its design.

The *Spirit of St. Louis* is a stock model with a few

Courtesy Wright Aeronautical Corp.

THE GREAT WRIGHT "WHIRLWIND" ENGINE WHICH CARRIED LINDBERGH TO VICTORY

A 200 horsepower, air-cooled, nine cylinder motor, in which every known device for safety and efficiency is incorporated. Captain Lindbergh cabled from Paris "Motor functioned perfectly

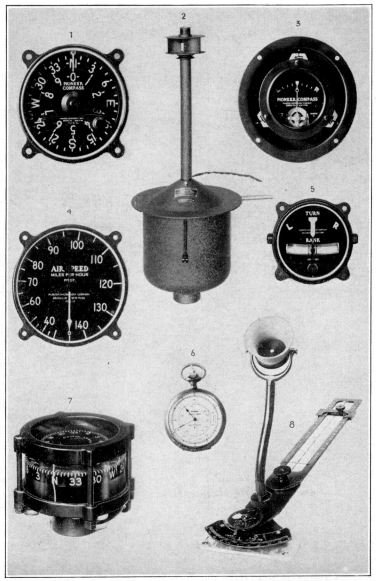

Courtesy Pioneer Instrument Co., Brooklyn, N. Y.

NAVIGATING INSTRUMENTS USED BY LINDBERGH

1, Controller, 2, Generator, 3, Indicator of Earth-inductor Compass. 4, Air Speed Indicator. 5, Turn and Bank Indicator. 6, Speed Timer for use with Speed and Drift Indicator. 7, Magnetic Compass. 8, Speed and Drift Indicator.

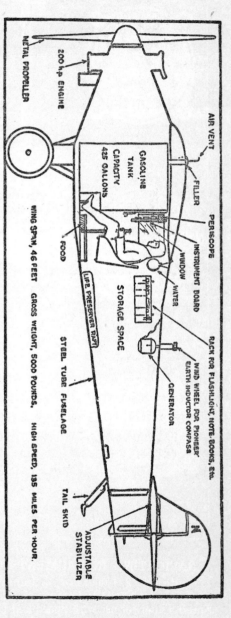

DIAGRAM OF THE "SPIRIT OF ST. LOUIS"

METAL PROPELLER

200 h.p. ENGINE

AIR VENT

FILLER

PERISCOPE

GASOLINE TANK CAPACITY 425 GALLONS

INSTRUMENT BOARD

WINDOW

WATER

RACK FOR FLASHLIGHT, NOTE-BOOKS, Etc.

WIND WHEEL FOR PIONEER EARTH INDUCTOR COMPASS

FOOD

STORAGE SPACE

LIFE PRESERVER RAFT

GENERATOR

WING SPAN, 46 FEET   GROSS WEIGHT, 5000 POUNDS.   HIGH SPEED, 135 MILES PER HOUR.

STEEL TUBE FUSELAGE

TAIL SKID

ADJUSTABLE STABILIZER

This longitudinal cross-section of Lindbergh's plane shows clearly the mechanism of the "little bus" that carried him in one hop from New York to Paris. The ship is a monoplane with a wing spread of 46 feet and a length of 28 feet. The operator sits in a wicker chair in a completely enclosed cockpit. On either side is a door with a window which could be readily opened. There is another window overhead, but the forward view is entirely cut off by the big gasoline tank holding 448 gallons, which is mounted just behind the motor. An optical instrument with reflecting prisms, known as a periscope, permitted Lindbergh to look ahead if necessary, but as the window and instruments gave all needed information, the periscope was little used. The instruments included temperature gauge, oil pressure gauge, tachometer, altimeter, turn and bank indicator, air speed and drift indicator, speed timer, and clock.

improvements made to meet the extra demands of an extended flight. The wings of Lindbergh's plane were made somewhat larger than those of the regular Ryan plane, to give it greater lifting power. The stream-lines were improved and refined to cut resistance to the minimum.

COCKPIT INCLOSED IN FUSELAGE

The cockpit is entirely inclosed in the fuselage so that the plane appears to be flying itself. It is beau-tifully streamlined and offers the least possible resist-ance to the wind, which gives it a high top speed, believed to be about 135 miles an hour when flown with a wide-open throttle.

Superficially the plane resembles the Bellanca plane, because it has struts from the wing to the bottom of the fuselage, deeply streamlined. But the Bellanca struts are made in the form of wings, so that they add to the lift of the plane, and also the fuselage is built with a convex curve on the top which helps lift some of its own weight. The Ryan wing also is of one piece, straight across the top, and fastened to the top of the fuselage, whereas the Bellanca wings are in two pieces, joined to the top outside edge of the fuselage and tip-ping very slightly upward, so slightly that it is hardly perceptible.

The Ryan wing is built of wood, carefully braced and lightened as much as is consistent with safety and covered with fabric, "doped" and painted silver color. Where the struts join the wing and the body of the plane they are extremely well streamlined, offering the minimum wind resistance.

SAFER IN CRASH

The body of the plane also has unusually clean lines, from the nose which supports the motor, to the tail. Just back of the motor the bow of the plane is covered with polished duralumin, which shines in the sunlight, and from the point where the wing joins the fuselage aft to the rudder the surface is covered with fabric also painted silver color. The fuselage frame is made of duralumin tubes welded together. It has to be of great strength to support the weight of the big tank just back of the engine and under the forward half of the wing. Back of this tank is the pilot's compartment, in a position that is as safe as possible in a crash or forced landing, because the weight of the tank goes forward.

In the Bellanca, the tank is back of the pilots, so that they are between it and the engine, if the plane dives into the ground.

COMPLETELY STREAMLINED

In order to streamline the plane as much as possible the usual cockpit, which permits the pilot to look forward over the wing, was abandoned, and the cockpit was dropped entirely inside the fuselage, making a tiny box in which Lindbergh sat cooped up in front of his instrument board. He was not as uncomfortable as would be imagined, because his wicker chair was placed far enough back so his long legs did not get unduly cramped as they rested on the rudder bars. But there was mighty little room for him to move about.

The odd construction of the cockpit made it impossible for him to look ahead in the usual way, so he had a periscope made so that he could push it out on the side when he wanted to see what was in front of him. It worked only on the left side, however. His only other vision was down on the sides from the tiny windows about level with his shoulders. An opening about an inch and a half square under the wing on the right side carried fresh air to the cockpit, so that he did not suffer from fumes of the gasoline tank and engine.

TEN MILES TO THE GALLON

With full load the plane has a cruising speed of approximately 105 miles an hour and a maximum speed of 123 miles. It carries 448 gallons of gasoline and 28 gallons of oil, estimated to be sufficient for a 4500 mile jump.

On his 2500 mile trip from San Diego, Calif., to New York, Lindbergh used less than 250 gallons of gasoline and the average consumption is computed at about 10 gallons an hour.

Its body of metal and wings of wood, the *Spirit of St. Louis* has a gross weight of 5150 pounds, the full load of gasoline and oil weighing 2745 pounds.

It carried no radio, but is equipped with a pneumatic raft for use in case of a forced descent at sea. The plane is equipped only with wheels and if landed on the water could not take off again.

The plane's gasoline tanks have been equipped with special petcocks so that the tanks can be quickly emptied of their gasoline in case of a forced landing at sea, the tanks thus being available as floaters for the craft.

THE ENGINE

Rivaling in importance the plane itself is the engine on whose reliability and stamina depended not only the success of the flight, but the very life of the pilot. It seems a far cry from the days of the first flights of the Wright brothers, who were compelled to build their own motor to obtain one which would develop eight horsepower with a weight of 200 pounds, to the perfection of the Wright "Whirlwind" Model J-5C engine developing 200 horsepower at 1800 revolutions per minute with a weight of 508 pounds, yet all this has been accomplished in twenty-five years. This engine consists of nine air-cooled cylinders, of $4\frac{1}{2}$-inch bore by $5\frac{1}{2}$ stroke, fixed radially about the moving crank shaft which has but one crank throw. There are two magnetos for ignition, either or both of which can be used. The oil, of which 28 gallons were carried, is pumped at high pressure to the cylinders and all bearing surfaces and there is also a pump for the gasoline to maintain constant pressure at the carburetor.

FAITH IN MOTOR WON

Ed Mulligan is the Wright Whirlwind motor expert who on that historic Friday morning told Captain Charles Lindbergh that his engine would take him to Paris. It did, as all the world knows, but not for the reason that most people think it did, Mulligan insists.

Most persons would tell you that the motor is the finest air-cooled engine in the 200-horsepower engine class which America has developed. They would cite the 2,400,000 miles of flying the motors have made without a forced landing.

As expert for the company, a highly paid technician on whom the company relies when a difficult job is in prospect, Mulligan knows all about the excellence of the motor which took Lindbergh over the 3800 miles of land and ocean in thirty-three and one-half hours, too.   But he has his own private hunch as well.

It was faith which carried Lindbergh to Paris, he says.   That Mulligan instilled that faith in Lindbergh is evidenced by what the daring pilot said when he arrived in Paris.

"I knew my bus would carry me," said Lindbergh, "and the bus seemed to know my confidence in it and went on purring fine."

That's all that Mulligan wants—faith.

While Lindbergh was still in the air Saturday morning somewhere over the Atlantic Ocean, Mulligan was elated over the way everyone was pulling for the "kid."

"It'll put him over," declared Mulligan, who is by nature just a little harder boiled than tempered steel, "if they only keep pulling for him and believing the kid'll make it.

"I guess I've been on hand at every long-distance flight pulled off in this country, and it's all a question of confidence in the motor.   My job is to get the flier to feel that all he has to do is to feed that engine gas and oil and it'll keep going.   If he gets that idea and believes in it, the thing is a cinch.

"The kid believed it, and as long as everyone else does, he's sitting pretty."

Mulligan can tell you detailed and convincing stories how this pilot could keep aloft with the same engine which would quit cold the minute another pilot's hand touched the throttle. The motor will work forever, Mulligan believes, "but not unless you have faith."

"Talk about women being touchy," said Mulligan, "they haven't got it in them to be as finicky as motors. You got to be the right man to handle 'em right."

Next to the amazing mechanical efficiency of the engine is the remarkable feat of navigation performed by Lindbergh. Ships have found their way from port to port since time immemorial and the art of navigation has grown to such perfection that it is possible for the captain to tell his position at any moment with remarkable accuracy. Aërial navigation, however, presents different problems. The pilot and navigator has little room or time for intricate mathematical calculations but must devote the major portion of his attention to the flying of the ship. His eye must frequently visit the oil pressure and oil temperature gauges; the engine revolution counter or tachometer tells him whether the motor is functioning properly; the air speed meter is another check on the proper performance of the ship. As a consequence, Lindbergh did not use the sextant, which is the navigating instrument of seamen, but depended on dead reckoning, which is simply an accurate estimate of the direction and distance flown, to keep on his course.

The navigator's first step in preparing for such a trip would be to lay out on a chart of the Atlantic Ocean a great circle route from New York to Paris. (A great circle is the shortest distance between two points on the earth's surface.) He then plots checking points, usually at 300 mile intervals, and establishes the course to be steered from each point. His initial course of departure is true 53° 51′, but this must be corrected for variation and deviation of the compass before the true course can be set. At each point in the voyage the course must be changed to follow the Great Circle, so that accurate knowledge of position is highly essential. Furthermore, the direction of the wind has a very decided effect on the course of the plane, so that it is necessary to use a speed and drift indicator to obtain the true course over land or water and correct the compass course accordingly.

THE EARTH-INDUCTOR COMPASS

Lindbergh gave much of the credit for his remarkable feat of navigation in striking the Irish coast within three miles of the point at which he had planned to reach it, to the Pioneer Earth-Inductor Compass with which the *Spirit of St. Louis* was equipped. The combination of a remarkable new compass and the unerring instinct of a youth who knew direction to the dot, are looked upon today as the answer to the question: How did Lindbergh find his way across?

The compass was described in detail by Commander R. D. Weyerbacher, builder of the *Shenandoah*, and chief engineer in the U. S. Naval Aircraft factory at the Navy Yard. And with the explanation one understands why "Lucky," in Paris, said:

"It wasn't all luck. I had a wonderful compass with me and with it I scarcely got off my route at all."

"The earth-inductor compass, developed by the Bureau of Standards at the request of the National Advisory Committee for Aëronautics, came out in

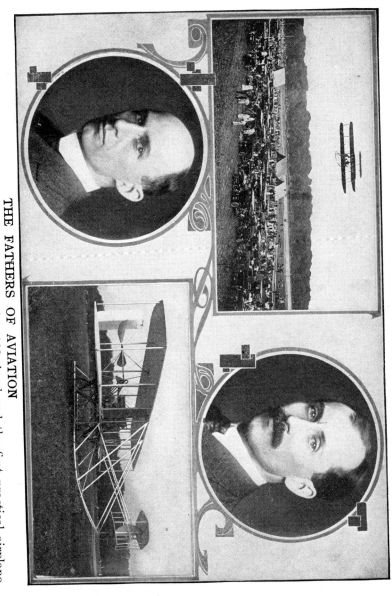

THE FATHERS OF AVIATION

The famous Wright brothers, whose experiments in 1903 developed the first practical airplane, shown here. At the left is Wilbur W. Wright and at the right is Orville W. Wright.

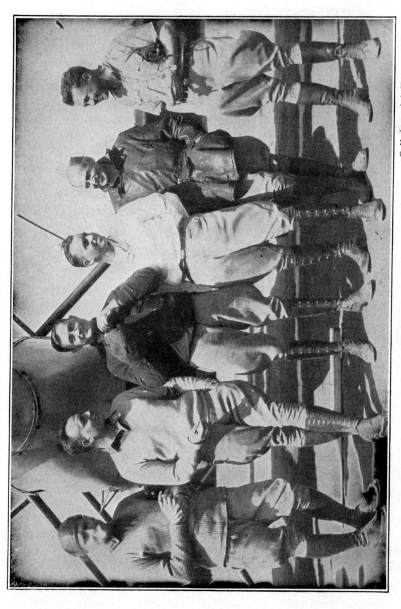

THE UNITED STATES "ROUND THE WORLD" FLIERS

© *Underwood & Underwood, N. Y.*

On the epoch-making journey of the three great planes which flew around the world, the officers in this picture were in command. From left to right: Lieutenants Wade, Arnold, Smith, Ogden,

1923," Commander Weyerbacher said. "It is manufactured by the Pioneer Instrument Company, Brooklyn, and was invented by Dr. Paul R. Heyl and Dr.
Lyman J. Briggs, of the bureau. Previously several had
been tried out, but proved impractical for general use.

"The device is essentially a magnetic compass. It
is actuated by the force of the earth's magnetic field
(the earth is, to illustrate, like a minute nervous
system threaded with an infinite number of magnetic
lines of force).

"It differs from the ordinary magnetic compass,"
the commander continued, "in that the magnetized
needles are not employed to detect the direction of the
earth's magnetic lines of force."

Now, then, how does it work?

It operates by means of the earth's magnetic field
just as does the old and familiar needle compass, but
it is far more accurate. The needle compass can
seldom be read to greater accuracy than one degree
when it is stationary, and when mounted on an airplane, which vibrates while the engine is running, it
cannot be read to greater accuracy than two degrees.
Moreover, it must be mounted in front of the pilot and
therefore is near the engine and subject to magnetic
disturbances of the ignition and the great mass of iron.

SETS COURSE

The earth-inductor compass is subject to the same
magnetic disturbances, but it is mounted in the tail
of the plane, far from the engine, and so the disturbances are reduced to a negligible factor. It can be
read to one-quarter of a degree.

The compass consists of an armature wound as in an electric generator and revolved by the wind. The magnetic field of the earth acts as a field for the compass and makes it in fact an electric generator. When the brushes on the armature are set due north and south no magnetic lines of the field are cut and no current generated, but when the brushes are turned from this position, due to a change in the direction of the plane, a current is generated and is carried by wires to the instrument board, where an indicator needle swings over a scale marked to show that the plane has swung to the right or the left.

When the pilot sees that the needle has swung from the center position he turns his plane till the needle is again in the center and thus returns to his course. If he wishes to change his course he turns the controller of the compass, also mounted on the instrument board, to the desired direction. This swings the brushes on the compass out of their north and south position, and consequently displaces the indicator needle. Then he turns the ship till the needle is in the center, which shows he is on the new course.

TURN INDICATOR

This was the vital instrument of those used by Lindbergh, but others are also essential. A turn indicator shows with even greater accuracy than the compass when the ship turns even a fraction of a degree from a straight course. This instrument is made with a small gyroscope revolving at 14,000 revolutions per minute by means of the rush of air past the plane.

A bank indicator shows when the plane is banked

properly on turns, for an airplane must tip toward the inside of a curve, just as does a bicycle rider, or it will "skid." This indicator is simply a steel ball in a glass tube filled with alcohol, and it remains in the center when the plane is set at the proper angle, but flies off to the side if the plane starts to "skid."

A drift meter measures the angle at which a plane is traveling from its course because of a cross wind.

DRIFT INDICATOR

Wind, of course, is simply a body of air in motion, and a plane, carried along in this moving mass, instead of going straight, in relation to a course laid on the ground or on a map, may travel diagonally. The drift meter is a simple arm with a peep sight and a calibrated scale set to move in a horizontal plane. The pilot looks through the sight and along the arm at objects on the ground. If the plane has any lateral movement, or drift, objects on the ground will cross the arm at an angle. But if the arm is moved into such position at an angle to the side of the plane that objects move straight along the arm as the plane flies past them, then the arm indicates the true direction of flight.

The pilot can then turn his plane and fly at an angle into the wind so that, while his plane points off his course, his true flight, due to wind as well as the propeller, lies along the course which he wishes to take.

This angle of deviation is read accurately on the drift meter and, by displacing the control of the earth-inductor compass to a corresponding degree, the plane is kept on its course.

While the precision of these instruments is great, they are by no means perfectly accurate. Skill is required to read the scales accurately. Navigators and air pilots therefore emphasize the points that, while Lindbergh had these aids to navigation, his success lay in the good use he made of them, and not solely in the instruments themselves or in any of his so-called luck.

CHAPTER XXVII

This Narrowing World

IT is no longer true that "East is East, and West is West, and never the twain shall meet." Lindbergh has brought the Old World and the New within less than a day and a half's reach of each other. This young American eagle, who, on a day in May, soared up from the far western coast of the United States, and, with a brief pause at St. Louis and New York, followed the Great Circle out over the Atlantic and descended upon Paris, graphically and dramatically illustrated the enormous strides that have been taken in overcoming distances on the earth.

Looking back over the centuries, we can see the steady narrowing of the world through the instrumentality of, first, the sailboat, then the railroad train, the steamship, the electric telegraph and cable and telephone, the radio, the airship and the airplane—these have been the successive steps taken to bring the peoples of the world closer together.

The development of transportation is synonymous with the development of civilization. Man was his own burden bearer originally, then he trained the animals to carry him and his wares. The horse, the ass, the mule, the camel, the llama, the elephant, even the dog, all of these and others became man's helper in narrowing the distances between points on the land. Long ages passed before the oceans were crossed and

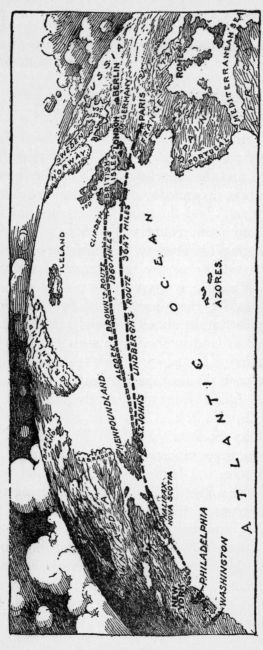

ROUTES OF TWO PIONEER TRANSATLANTIC FLIERS

Captain John Alcock and Lieut. Arthur W. Brown flew from St. John's, Newfoundland to Ireland in 1919, in 16 hours 12 minutes. The heavy line shows the route taken by Captain Lindbergh in 1927 in the first flight from New York to Paris.

the earth was circumnavigated, though men have
used crude boats on rivers and inland seas from time
immemorial.

THE DEVELOPMENT OF TRANSPORTATION

Earlier than the times covered by history the ancient
Briton and Gaul paddled his "coracle" of skin stretched
on wickerwork, and the American Indian his birch-bark
and dugout canoe, up and down the rivers. All these
(except the dugout) had the great advantage that the
traveler could go across country but slightly impeded
by simply slinging his boat to his back and passing
through the woods or across the prairies (portage).
In the early Mississippi days before the steamboat
(and since then, for that matter) the flat boat and
the raft with its house aboard floated calmly along
"Old Muddy," to land in the lower stretches with its
freight of furs, hides, bacon, etc. Few took the trouble
to pole or tow back the floatage upstream.

Then came James Rumsey and the Marquis de
Jouffroy and John Fitch (1790) and Robert Fulton
(1807) and John Stevens, and the river, as well as
navigation, was revolutionized. The Hudson got its
Clermont and soon the Hudson and the Sound were
both aswarm with a fleet built by Fulton & Livingston,
while John Stevens & Sons had their flotilla on the
Delaware and Connecticut rivers. The races on the
"Father of Waters" gave the famous flat-bottomed
Robert E. Lee, the *Natchez*, and other craft the name
of "flying palaces." It should be said that the excitement was often increased by a sky flight when the
overpressed boilers "gave out."

Some seven thousand years ago the Egyptians used single-masted ships to carry merchandise to the Nile—ivory, gold, Khesit wood, incense, resin, cosmetic paint, leopard skins, monkeys, greyhounds, and other "mixed" cargoes.   More popular in our minds is the Homeric Argosy of a later day.   The famous Phœnician trading skippers of a still later period come to memory, also their great colonial port of Carthage.   In the barbaric North the Vikings' ships (deckless) reached Greenland and perhaps New England.   Venetian and Genoese ships, later on, carried treasures (silks, spices, precious stone, etc.) from India and Cathay (China).   The Atlantic Ocean, however, still defied intruders until the intrepid Columbus, then da Gama, Magellan, and Drake, disclosed that the world was round!

The European and American thirst for tea made speed and security of cargo urgent, and comfort for the increasing number of passengers was called for—they produced the East Indiaman.   Sails were on a thousand seas.

FROM SAILBOAT TO STEAMSHIP

Then, to undermine the sailing vessels came Bell, of Glasgow, and John Fitch and Robert Fulton, of America; and the *Comet*, plying on Scotch and Irish waters, at the same time as the *Clermont*, paddled their way into marine history.

In 1819 the Atlantic was crossed by the first steamship, the *Savannah*, from the port of that name, in Georgia, to Liverpool; propelled by sail as well as by steam.   In 1838 the *Sirius* and the *Great Western* may be said to have established transatlantic traffic.

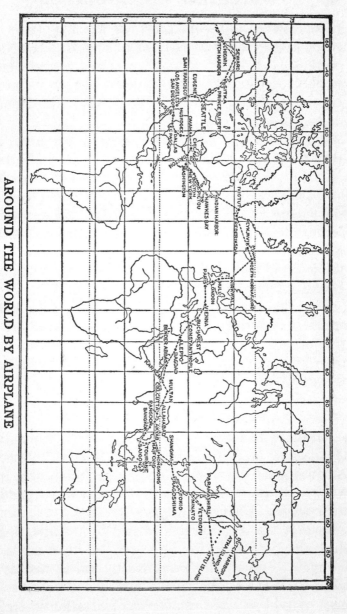

AROUND THE WORLD BY AIRPLANE

Chart of the epochal air voyage around the world made by American fliers in 1924.

The process of narrowing the world was well on its way.

Although in 1838 the *Sirius* and the *Great Western* successfully made the journey from England to America, yet five years before that date, Canadian enterprise accomplished the feat of bridging the Atlantic Ocean with a little vessel propelled wholly by steam. This was the *Royal William*, whose beautiful model was exhibited at the British Naval Exhibition in London, where she attracted the attention and curiosity of the first seamen of the Empire. She left Quebec for London, under steam, on August 4, 1833, and made the passage in twenty-five days. Her supply of coal was given as "254 chaldrons"—the equivalent of over 330 tons. Her captain, John McDougall, spoke no less proudly of the *Royal William* than did Charles Lindbergh of the *Spirit of St. Louis*. Said the doughty McDougall, "She is justly entitled to be considered the first steamer that crossed the Atlantic by steam, *having steamed the whole way across.*"

Important as were the *Savannah* and the *Royal William* in maritime annals, it was not until 1838 that the successful passages of two memorable vessels from England to America fairly established the era of what has been called the Atlantic steam-ferry. These ships were respectively the *Sirius* and the *Great Western*. The former was a craft of about 700 tons burden, with engines of three hundred and twenty horsepower: she sailed from Cork on the 4th of April, 1838, bound for New York. The latter vessel was a steamer of 1340 tons, with engines of four hundred and forty horsepower, and sailed from Bristol, April 8, in the

same year, also bound for New York.   The *Sirius*
arrived off Sandy Hook on Sunday, April 22; but
going aground, she did not get into the North River
until the following morning.   When it was known
that she had arrived, New York became, as one writer
of the time expressed it, "instantly agitated with excitement."   This excitement was augmented when it
heard that the *Great Western* was also nearing the port.
It may be of interest to quote here the description of
how New York, in those early days of Atlantic passages,
received the voyagers.   The account is taken from the
Journal of Commerce:

NEW YORK'S ENTHUSIASM IN 1838

"The news spread like wildfire through the city, and
the river became literally dotted all over with boats
conveying the curious to and from the stranger.
There seemed to be a universal voice in congratulation,
and every visage was illuminated with delight.   A
tacit conviction seemed to pervade every bosom that
a most doubtful problem had been satisfactorily solved;
visions of future advantage to science, to commerce, to
moral philosophy, began to float before the 'mind's
eye'; curiosity to travel through the old country, and
to inspect ancient institutions, began to stimulate the
inquiring.

"Whilst all this was going on, suddenly there was
seen over Governor's Island a dense black cloud of
smoke spreading itself upward, and betokening another
arrival.   On it came with great rapidity, and about
three o'clock in the afternoon its cause was made fully
manifest to the accumulated multitudes at the Battery.

It was the steamship *Great Western*, of about 1600 tons burden (*sic*) [the difference probably lies between the net and the gross tonnage], under the command of Lieutenant Hoskins, R.N.   She had left Bristol on the 8th inst., and on the 23d was making her triumphant entry into the port of New York.   This immense moving mass was propelled at a rapid rate through the waters of the Bay; she passed swiftly and gracefully round the *Sirius*, exchanging salutes with her, and then proceeded to her destined anchorage in the East River.   If the public mind was stimulated by the arrival of the *Sirius*, it became almost intoxicated with delight upon view of the superb *Great Western*.   The latter vessel was only fourteen clear days out; and neither vessel had sustained a damage worth mentioning, notwithstanding that both had to encounter very heavy weather.   The *Sirius* was spoken with on the 14th of April in latitude 45° north, longitude 37° west. The *Great Western* was spoken on the 15th of April in latitude 46° 26′ north, longitude 37° west.   At these respective dates the *Great Western* had run 1305 miles in seven days from King Road; and the *Sirius* 1305 miles in ten days from Cork.   The *Great Western* averaged 186½ miles per day, and the *Sirius* 130½ miles; *Great Western* gained on the *Sirius* fifty-six miles per day.   The *Great Western* averaged seven and three-quarter miles per hour; the *Sirius* barely averaged five and a half miles per hour."

The success of these two vessels may be said to have completely established steam as a condition of the transatlantic navigation of the future.   "In October, 1838," says Lindsay, in his *History of Merchant Ship-*

ping, "Sir John Tobin, a well-known merchant of Liverpool, seeing the importance of the intercourse now rapidly increasing between the Old and New Worlds, despatched on his own account a steamer to New York. She was built at Liverpool, after which place she was named, and made the passage outwards in sixteen and a half days. It was now clearly proved that the service could be performed, not merely with profit to those who engaged in it, but with a regularity and speed which the finest description of sailing vessels could not be expected to accomplish. If any doubts still existed on these important points, the second voyage of the *Great Western* set them at rest, she having on this occasion accomplished the outward passage in fourteen days sixteen hours, bringing with her the advices of the fastest American sailing ships which had sailed from New York long before her, and thus proving the necessity of having the mails in future conveyed by steamers."

In fact, as early as October, 1838, the British government, being satisfied of the superiority of steam packets over sailing ships, issued advertisements inviting tenders for the conveyance of the American mails by the former class of vessels. The owners of the *Great Western*, big with confidence in the reputation of that ship, applied for the contract; but, not a little to their chagrin, it was awarded to Mr. (afterwards Sir Samuel) Cunard, who as far back as 1830 had proposed the establishment of a steam mail service across the Atlantic. The terms of the original contract were, that for the sum of fifty-five thousand pounds per annum, Messrs. Cunard, Burns, and MacIver should supply three ships suitable for the purpose, and accomplish two voyages each month between Liverpool and the United States, leaving England at certain periods; but shortly afterwards it was deemed more expedient to name fixed dates of departure on both sides of the Atlantic Ocean. Subsequently, another ship was required to be added to the service, and the amount of the subsidy was raised to eighty-one thousand pounds a year. The steam mail service between Liverpool, Halifax, and Boston was regularly established in 1840, the first vessel engaged in it being the *Britannia*, the pioneer ship of the présent Cunard line.

We get an admirable idea of what these early steamships were from Dickens's account of this same *Britannia*, which was the vessel he crossed to America in on his first visit to this country in 1842. In one of his letters to John Forster, describing a storm they were overtaken by, he unconsciously reflects the wondering regard with which the world still viewed the triumphant achievements of the marine engine. "For two or three hours," he writes, "we gave it up as a lost thing. This was not the exaggerated apprehension of a landsman merely. The head engineer, who had been in one or the other of the Cunard vessels since they began running, had never seen such stress of weather; and I afterwards heard Captain Hewitt say that nothing but a steamer, and one of that strength, could have kept her course and stood it out. A sailing vessel must have beaten off and driven where she would; while through all the fury of that gale they actually made fifty-four miles headlong through the tempest, straight on end, not varying their track in the least."

What would the skipper of one of the modern "Atlantic greyhounds" think of such a feat? And more interesting speculation still, what must Dickens himself have thought of the performances he lived to witness as against this astonishing accomplishment on the part of the old *Britannia?*

There exists a tendency to ridicule the early steamers as they appear in portraits, with their huge paddle boxes; tall, thin, dog-eared funnels; and heavily-rigged masts, as though their engines were regarded as quite auxiliary to their sail power, and by no means to be relied upon. Contrasted with some of the leviathans of the present day, the steamers of half a century ago are no longer calculated to strike an awe into the beholder; but, in truth, some very fine vessels were built while the marine engine was still quite in its infancy.

From this time ocean steamers multiplied rapidly. One after another of the now famous shipping firms sprang up, beginning with the Cunard and the Peninsular and Oriental lines, culminating in such monster steamships as the *Leviathan*, with a registered tonnage of 59,957 and a length of 907 feet 6 inches, and the *Majestic*, 56,551 tons, and 915 feet 5 inches long.

Thus beginning with the *Savannah*, increasingly great ocean liners have swept to and fro over the turbulent ocean, bringing the peoples of the two hemispheres in closer contact.

OTHER AGENCIES IN NARROWING THE WORLD

The mighty locomotive has done its splendid part also in bridging distances; so, too, have the electric locomotive, the trolley car, and the motor bus. The telegraph, telephone, and radio should be included in this brief view of distance bridgers.

But it is to the airplane that the greatest tribute must be paid for narrowing the planet. Even the fastest Atlantic Ocean passages, recorded by the Cunard liner *Mauretania*, were made in four days, ten hours, and fifty-one minutes, and in four days, thirteen hours, and forty-one minutes, in 1909. Lindbergh spanned New York and Paris between two sleeps.

"MY DECREPIT ITALIAN FRIEND"

CHAPTER XXVIII

The Trail Blazers of the Air

LINDBERGH and the flying machine grew up together. There is just a year or two of difference between their ages. It was in December, 1903, that the Wright brothers, of Dayton, Ohio, succeeded in making their first practical flight in a double-decked, motor-driven aëroplane, or "aërostat" as it was variously called. So the airplane is just eighteen months younger than Lindbergh, who was born in February, 1902.

Long before that year, however, men had dreamed of the time when they would conquer the air and bid defiance to whatever winds may blow. At first came the application of power to the balloon, and among the pioneer experimenters was Santos-Dumont, who thrilled the world with his exploits in a cylindrical gasbag, pointed at each end, and carrying a car with driving and steering apparatus below—an invention which Count Zeppelin and others have developed into the beautiful and powerful dirigibles which sweep over oceans and continents as the *R-34* and the *Los Angeles* and other great ships of the air have done.

But wonderful as are these masters of the air, it is the much smaller, but much faster and much more easily controlled aëroplane, the "heavier-than-air" machine, that has captured the world's interest.

WITH WINGS LIKE A BIRD

That man should be able to fly like a bird, provided he had wings, was the first thought; and with manufactured wings, many brave men sacrificed their lives in their attempts to ape the bird.   Dr. Otto Lilienthal was one of these martyrs to science; with his gliders he had made a number of demonstrations, but he met with disaster in 1896, when he was caught by a sudden gust of wind, lost control of his wings, and was fatally injured.

Within recent years the glider, built more after the fashion of a modern airplane, but without engine, has been revived, and with some success.   Such a flying machine, however, could be of no practical or commercial value.   Advantage has to be taken of air currents, and sustained flight is impossible.

It is the plane with the motor that has proved its practical quality and is rapidly becoming of immense importance in the industrial world.

TRAGEDY LEAVES ITS RED TRAIL ON THE AIRWAYS

Before the airplane as we know it today had been developed, many men made the supreme sacrifice to prove their faith in their invention—and the recent loss of Nungesser and Coli, just before Lindbergh started his flight to Paris, is one more tragic illustration of the risks the birdman must still take.

According to the records, the honor of being the first to design a practical motor-driven airplane was an Englishman by the name of Stringfellow, who as far back as 1868 won a prize for his machine at the Crystal Palace in London.   Steam was the driving power.

Cayley and Henson, in England, and many other inventors, added their quota to the science.

It was not, however, until the Wright brothers, in 1903, made their first successful flight that the airplane definitely "arrived."

Before them, Hiram Maxim had exhibited a machine that was able to lift itself from the ground and make a fair speed in the air.   S. P. Langley also built an airplane that made a speed of about twenty-four miles an hour.   Both used steam engines.   Berliner and other pioneers joined the roll of investigators.

THE COMING OF THE WRIGHT BROTHERS

Then came the Wrights—and success.   It was at Kitty Hawk, North Carolina, on December 17, 1903, that Wilbur Wright made his history-making flight, the forerunner of a million others.

The difficulties which the Wright brothers faced may be classed in three groups: (1) those relating to the construction of the sustaining wings; (2) those relating to the generation and application of the power required to drive the machine through the air; and (3) those relating to the balancing and steering of the machine after it is actually in flight.

To quote from Wilbur Wright's own story: "My active interest in aëronautical problems dates back to the death of Lilienthal, in 1896.   We figured that Lilienthal had in five years' time spent only five hours in the air, yet Lilienthal, with this brief practice, was remarkably successful in meeting the fluctuations and eddies of wind gusts.   It seemed feasible to practice by the hour, instead of the second, by building a machine which would be sustained at a speed of eighteen miles an hour and then finding a locality where winds of this velocity were common.   With these conditions a rope attached to the machine to keep it from floating back with the wind would give us the same results as if we had a machine driven forward by a motor in a calm."

He and his brother found, according to the accepted Lilienthal tables of air pressure on curved surfaces, that they would need a machine spreading two hundred square feet and that winds of the sort they wished were common along the Atlantic coast.   When the winds were low, it was their plan to glide from the sandhills.

They concluded that tails of size were an impediment.   Also it seemed reasonable that if the body of the operator could be placed horizontally, only one square foot instead of five would be exposed to the wind.   Other experimenters, like Pilcher, Lilienthal, and Chanute, had been upright.

Then the method of control used by Lilienthal, which consisted in shifting the body, did not seem quick or effective enough; so the Wrights contrived a system consisting of two large surfaces on the Chanute double-decked plan, and a smaller surface placed directly in front, at a short distance, in such a position that the action of the wind upon it would counterbalance the effect of the travel of the center pressure on the main surface.

AT KITTY HAWK

With these plans the Wright brothers proceeded, in the summer of 1900, to Kitty Hawk, North Carolina, a little settlement located on the strip of land that separates Albermarle Sound from the Atlantic Ocean. Owing to the impossibility of obtaining suitable material for a two hundred square foot machine, they were compelled to make it only one hundred sixty-five square feet.

They turned their attention to gliding from the top of Kill Devil hill, a sand dune about one hundred feet high. Although landings were made while moving at speeds of more than twenty miles per hour, neither machine nor operator suffered injury.

THE GASOLINE MOTOR

Experiments were continued in 1901, 1902, and the earlier portion of 1903, culminating in the construction of a motor which they placed under the operator sufficiently to the rear to retain the center of gravity in its proper position according to their previous designs. A screw fan propeller was geared on a line to the rear, and a second one placed underneath the motor to serve to lift the machine, as the first propeller was meant to drive it.

The motor was their own gasoline type, and anything new that was introduced had already been suggested by their previous experiments.

Early in December they began to look forward to the day of trial. The weather was not propitious, but on the 17th the wind was blowing about twenty-one miles an hour, and the pilot took his place in the machine for a trial from the big hill. First, the lifting propeller was started, and facing the wind the machine rose easily and gracefully to the height of about sixty feet, and when the rear propeller began to hum and

14

the lifting propeller to slow down, the first flying machine sailed into the wind and traversed easily a distance of half a mile down the dunes.

Wilbur Wright did not live to see Lindbergh's superb flight—he died in 1912—but he spoke prophetically when he said at the time:

"Our experiments are not yet completed, but we feel confident of delivering to the world in no great stretch of time a completely practical flying-machine for everyday use."

OTHER TRAIL BLAZERS

There were other trail blazers whose names are famous in the annals of aviation. Among the French enthusiasts who took up the study were Louis Bleriot, Captain Louis Ferber, Ernest Archdeacon, and later the Voisin brothers and Santos-Dumont, the Brazilian aëronaut and sportsman who had been the earliest to construct a navigable balloon and later experimented with heavier-than-air craft.

In 1905 the Wright brothers flew $24\frac{1}{2}$ miles in 38 minutes and 3 seconds, at Dayton, Ohio. The following year, 1906, Santos-Dumont made the first public flight in Europe, in a box-kite type of plane, driven by a light gasoline engine. In 1907 Henri Farman made the first circular flight (1093 yards) in Europe, at Issy, France, and two years later, at Ghent, Belgium, Farman flew with a passenger 1360 yards, making the first public passenger flight; in May, 1908, he made the first cross-country flight, from Chalons to Rheims. In December of the same year Wilbur Wright flew $77\frac{1}{2}$ miles in 2 hours, 20 minutes, at Le Mans, France.

England also had become interested in aëronautics, and on December 31, 1908, at Farnborough, Hampshire, S. F. Cody flew 189 miles in 4 hours 47 minutes, winning the British Empire Michelin Prize.

One of the first to congratulate Lindbergh on his New York-to-Paris flight was Louis Bleriot, whose flight from Calais to Dover, across the English Channel, July 25, 1909, was little less spectacular in its day than the Lone Eagle's 3600-mile hop over the Atlantic. Bleriot blazed a new trail, and now passengers daily fly the shuttle between Paris and London.

In 1910 Louis Paulhan flew from London to Manchester, with one stop, winning the *Daily Mail's* £10,000 prize.

Glenn H. Curtiss, American designer of aircraft, flew from Albany to New York, with two stops, May 29, 1910. It was Curtiss who designed the motors for the dirigibles for Captain T. S. Baldwin, 1907–09, including the motor for the first dirigible accepted by the United States Government.

LINDBERGH'S PROPHECY

The years since 1910 have been crowded with aëronautic achievements: flights across the continent; flights across the Atlantic; flights to the North Pole and (by airship) from Norway over the top of the world to Alaska; Rodgers' flight to Hawaii from San Francisco in 1925; Cobham's flight from London to Melbourne and back, with various stops; the four-continent flight of Commander de Pinedo, of Italy; the around-the-world flight by American aviators; and many other flying feats that have brought nearer the prophesy of Captain Lindbergh that "within ten years airplanes will be flying regularly over the Atlantic."

As a trail blazer, Charles Lindbergh, the twenty-five-year-old air-mail pilot, did something more than merely fly from New York to Paris. He did something far greater. He fired the imagination of mankind and evoked all that was best in men's hearts and minds. In a day of none-too-good international feeling he erased rancor and suspicion, lighted a flame of good will, and, as one writer expressed it, "started a clean breeze around the world."

IS THERE A SPEED LIMIT FOR FLYING?

To the question as to how fast man will eventually fly, the record holders reply that physically they have received no indication of the limit. Scientists and designers, basing conclusions on fixed formulæ, set the absolute theoretical limit at 480 miles an hour, without consideration for such handicaps as fast landing speeds and controllability. They point out that such a plane would resemble a winged projectile, with wings so short they would be only 9 square feet in area on either side.

CHAPTER XXIX

Chamberlin Follows Lindbergh

LINKED with the exploit of Lindbergh is the flight of the Bellanca plane, the *Columbia*, which was piloted across the Atlantic by Clarence D. Chamberlin and in which Charles A. Levine was a passenger and who sometimes relieved Chamberlin as pilot. The *Columbia* had been one of the entrants for the Orteig New York-to-Paris prize of $25,000, but differences between Mr. Levine and pilots he had selected to accompany Chamberlin, had postponed the attempt. On Saturday, June 4, the long-delayed dash of the Bellanca was made.

The flight was decided upon about midnight of Friday, June 3. Weather reports showed an area of westerly winds and no trace of oncoming storm that extended far into the Atlantic. Mystery for days had shrouded the double-seated Bellanca. Where was its destination? Who would fly with Chamberlin? These were questions that neither Levine nor Chamberlin would answer. It was generally reported that Mrs. Chamberlin would fly with her husband. To her Chamberlin said: "Let them think what they please. The truth is the name of my companion must remain a secret until we actually start."

It was six minutes after six on Saturday morning when the heavily laden Bellanca finally took to the air. For hours a crowd had lined the same runway that had been used by Lindbergh.   Levine, hatless and in dark blue street clothes, was beside Chamberlin throughout the preparations.   Mrs. Levine smilingly watched the gasoline being poured into the tanks and the storing of thirteen extra containers of gasoline in the plane.   She had no idea of the shocking sensation which she was to experience.   Mrs. Chamberlin saw to the provisioning of the ship, consisting of ten sandwiches of ham and chicken and a half-dozen oranges, these latter at the suggestion of Levine.

BOUND FOR EUROPE

Chamberlin, when all this had been done, climbed into the cockpit and beckoned to Levine.   The Brooklyn business man, whose business start came as a dealer in old metal during the War, climbed into the seat beside the pilot.   Mrs. Levine started toward the plane with a shade of anxiety upon her face.   John Carisi, expert mechanician, ran over to reassure her. "It was only a test run," he said.   Then he ran over to Chamberlin and hugged him.

The *Columbia* roared down the runway as newspapermen excitedly surrounded Mrs. Levine.

"Is your husband going with Chamberlin?" they asked.

Her gay smile flashed.

"Oh, no," she replied.   "They are only trying the plane."

To confirm her statement, the *Columbia*, which had reached the end of the runway, halted, and Chamberlin, handling it as deftly as a crack chauffeur might swing a racing car, taxied back to the start.   Again

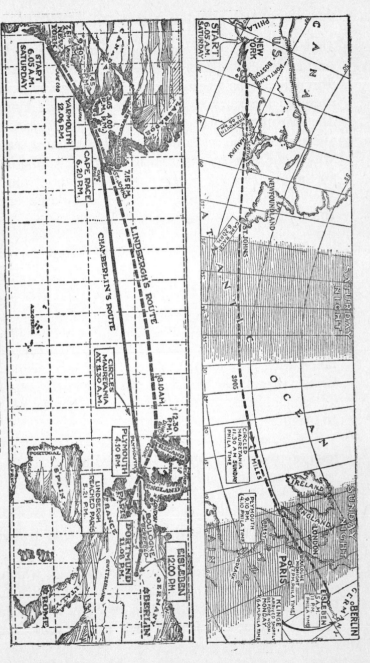

CHAMBERLIN'S ROUTE TO BERLIN

The upper illustration shows where Chamberlin and Levine met darkness on the ocean. Below is indicated the route of the *Spirit of St. Louis* and the Bellanca plane

the motor roared and rushed along the prepared path.
And now Mrs. Levine realized at last that her husband
was to be Chamberlin's companion.   Pallor overspread
her face.   She ran stumbling weakly after the rushing
winged chariot.   "Charles!" she called to him, and
then fell fainting into the arms of those who ran to her.

THE TAKE-OFF

The take-off was a marvel of skill.   Chamberlin
opened the motor wide, leveled down the tail of his
ship, and nosed its sharply upward.   It leaped as a
greyhound leaps over a hedge.   Expertly Chamberlin
leveled it after it had reached two hundred feet, and
sped over the neighboring fields.   Then he started to
climb into the very eye of the rising sun.   Up and up
he zoomed with a cluster of escorting planes from
Mitchell Field to bid him Godspeed.   Over the hills
and far away it went, disappearing at last in the film
of a white cloud upon the eastern horizon.

Almost at the beginning bad luck overtook him.
The ship had ventured barely one hundred miles when
comparison between the two compasses he carried
showed an alarming discrepancy.   The earth-inductor
compass, which had worked so perfectly for Lindbergh,
was not giving results to Chamberlin and Levine.   The
men in the cabin were up against it for navigation.
They could only rely upon the magnetic compass by
which ships chart their courses.

They remembered the thirteen extra tins of gasoline.
Levine had wanted John Carisi to put in either eleven
or fifteen.   Perhaps a hoodoo was commencing to work.
Up New England they turned for the long leg to Nova

Scotia. Head winds were encountered, and these held them back and exhausted the precious store of gasoline beyond their calculations. They reached Nova Scotia two and a half hours behind their schedule, and then boldly turned into the open sea with only the magnetic compass to guide them.

The need for food did not trouble them. Somewhere along the long route, neither could ever recall where, Chamberlin ate a sandwich and Levine an orange. Both drank freely from the thermos bottle of coffee. During the long run Levine dozed in his chair and upon waking relieved Chamberlin at the controls while the latter took a brief nap. Off the coast of Ireland they ran into more trouble. A storm lay dead ahead, and, heeding the advice of the United States Weather Bureau, they sped southward.

"We had plenty of luck," said Levine, later describing the flight, "but it was all bad."

CHAMBERLIN'S STORY OF THE FLIGHT

"Things went well with us at first," said Chamberlin, "but the end of the trip was dreadful. We had the wind with us and conditions held out fairly well until we got over the Irish Sea. Then we ran into a sleet storm that drove us higher and higher in what proved to be a useless effort to escape it.

"Finally we turned southward and spent some time over Boulogne looking for a landing place, but there was nothing in sight, so we kept on going. When we reached Belgium the fogs were so dense that we couldn't see a thing ahead. We saw water under us and of course we had to keep on.

"All the time we were heading east, hoping that our journey would bring us somewhere near Berlin. It was about 4 A. M., I guess, that we went over Dortmund. By this time we didn't know where we were. We went down only a few feet from the ground and I shouted to a group of workmen: 'Berlin! Berlin!' They looked very much surprised and I yelled again, pointing, ahead. They nodded and I supposed I was on the right course after all.

"We still kept running into fog banks and by now our gasoline was getting short. Over the channel we had thrown out our empty cans and a number of full ones in order to lighten the ship. Finally, as the fog was thickening, and our gas was about out, we decided to descend."

CIRCLING THE OCEAN LINER

They had circled the steamship *Mauretania* at 3.30 on Sunday afternoon, when they were about 360 miles west of the Scilly Islands.

News that the Bellanca plane *Columbia* had passed within twelve miles of the United States cruiser *Memphis* in its transatlantic flight from New York to an European destination, was the big event on Sunday not only for Captain Lindbergh but for the entire personnel of this cruiser which was taking the first New York-to-Paris flier back to America.

Lindburgh rushed to the bridge as soon as the wireless report was heard that the S. S. *Mauretania* had sighted the plane. He scanned the horizon hoping to catch a glimpse of the *Columbia*, but although the *Mauretania* at that time was still in sight, nothing whatever was seen of the fliers by the *Memphis*. This probably was due to the heavy mist.

It was midnight of Sunday when the Bellanca plane passed over Boulogne, France, and headed for Berlin. The gasoline was then running low. They were off the direct route to Berlin and flying in a dense fog. The last emergency tin of gasoline was poured into the tank and still there was no sight of the flares of Tempelhofer Airdrome, Berlin's great flying field.

Dawn came and the gasoline supply was at an end. Five o'clock on Monday morning Chamberlin brought the *Columbia* to earth in a field at Eisleben, Saxony, 110 miles southwest of Berlin.

IN SEARCH OF BERLIN

The first action of the fliers was to send for gasoline. A young man with a bicycle volunteered to find some. Sleepy citizens pointed out the general direction of Berlin. It was 9.35 in the morning when the *Columbia* again took to the air. Unfortunately they again were off the course to Berlin. They flew due east instead of northeast. The little store of gasoline was running low and its poor quality was producing engine trouble. Chamberlin saw directly ahead a field of oats. Here probably, he thought, should be a good landing. Only when he was a few feet above it did he discover the oats grew upon marshy ground. It was then too late. The front wheels stopped with a chuck in the mud. The big metal-sheaved propeller slapped the stuff in a black shower and finally broke. The *Columbia* was out of commission!

Chamberlin and Levine found themselves in the

tiny village of Klinge, 70 miles southeast of Berlin. The industrial town of Kottbus was near-by and there in an old-world comfortable inn they made a feast of spreewalld, eels, cucumbers, and other native dishes, washed down with white beer. It was a holiday but the stores were opened to supply them clean clothing. Levine's business suit was pressed. Both took warm baths and after a gallant reception by the townpeople, both slept the sleep of utter exhaustion.

The next day they flew to Berlin, where a series of receptions and honors came to them. President Von Hindenburg and other German officers hailed them as emissaries of peace. Lindbergh was first of all the world to wireless from the cruiser *Memphis* his hearty congratulations.

When Chamberlin decided upon his transatlantic flight in the Bellanca monoplane he did not say what his destination was to be, but said he would fly as far into Europe as his fuel would permit.

All sorts of guesses were made—Paris, Berlin, Rome, and other cities. The possibility that the Americans might reach Rome aroused the enthusiasm of the Italians, and elaborate preparations were made to guide the aviators in their flight.

Although disappointed at the decision of Chamberlin and Levine to fly to Germany instead of to Italy, the people of Rome hailed with enthusiasm the achievement of spanning the Atlantic from New York for the second time in a little more than a fortnight.

The Italian newspapers almost invariably referred to the Bellanca plane *Columbia* as a "magnificent product of Italian genius," this being a reference to the nationality of Giuseppe M. Bellanca, builder of the plane, who was born in Sicily.

Because of conflicting reports, the crowds which had waited all night for the arrival of the *Columbia* did not abandon hope until afternoon that the plane was flying toward Rome.

A report at three o'clock on the morning of June 6 that the plane was heading for Rome sent a rush of several hundred automobiles to the Ciampino Airfield, where a large throng had already gathered.

THE BELLANCA PLANE

Superficially, the Bellanca plane in which Chamberlin and Levine crossed the Atlantic, and the Ryan monoplane in which Lindbergh blazed the trail, are much alike. To the experienced eye of pilots, however, there are many things in the Bellanca which sets it apart— the lifting power of the struts for one thing, which is a secret of the designer, Giuseppe M. Bellanca.

Both planes are stock models of their respective builders, the Bellanca, or *Columbia*, having been constructed for use in the air-mail service. As far as instruments were concerned the planes were nearly duplicates, each carrying instruments made by the Pioneer Instrument Company of Brooklyn. The earth-inductor compass, to which Lindbergh gave instinted praise when he landed at Paris, was part of the Bellanca equipment.

Lindbergh flew without a radio set and so did Chamberlin and Levine. When the Bellanca was first preparing for the hop-off a radio set was part of the equipment. Later it was decided to abandon it; then a reconsideration caused the pilots to decide to take one along—a low power set for use only in emergency. Even this was dispensed with, however, when the plane finally got off.

HAD LOAD OF 5418 POUNDS

When the *Columbia* had climbed into the air a load of 5418 pounds was lifted, of which 1850 was her own weight.

Mr. Bellanca said the plane carried 455 gallons of gasoline, weighing 2757 pounds and that eighteen gallons of oil, weighing 135 pounds, were also stowed away in the tanks. A Very pistol, smoke bombs, flares, and cartridges were also aboard, according to Ugo d'Annunzio, son of the Italian aviator-poet, who watched the loading on behalf of the designer.

When the Lindbergh plane took off, the weight that went soaring into the air was 5150, approximately 300 pounds lighter than the Bellanca. The wing measurements of the two planes are virtually identical as far as length is concerned, each spanning about 46 feet. The wings of the Lindbergh plane are wider, however, giving it a wing spread of 320 cubic feet as against the Bellanca's spread of 272.

Both planes are the same in the department of power. Each is equipped with a nine-cylinder Wright whirlwind motor, weighing 500 pounds and capable of developing between 200 and 225 horsepower. The speed claimed for each is 130 miles an hour at maximum, while the Bellanca claims a cruising speed of 100 to 110 miles an hour. Lindbergh on his transatlantic flight averaged something like 107 miles an hour.

The fuselage of the Bellanca, which is shorter than that of the Ryan monoplane, is light gray in color, silvery in appearance, and the wings are a light lemon shade. The landing wheels are striped in red, white, and blue. The markings of the plane consist of the numeral "140" on either side and on the left side in red, white and blue is painted the head of "Miss Columbia."

Unlike Lindbergh's plane, which was so constructed that he could not see from it and had to use a periscope attachment to look ahead, the pilots in the Bellanca had a clear view on all sides. Chamberlin as pilot sat over a big gasoline tank as he watched the instrument board in front of him.

This board is a feature not found in Lindbergh's plane. It is fashioned like the control board of a power plant. It is three feet long and a foot wide. In even rows on the board are the air speed indicator, the double-dialed earth-inductor compass, altimeter, the tachometer, which registers the revolutions of the propeller, and the various oil and gasoline dials and gauges. Suspended in a duralumin fork from the mica roof of the cockpit was a magnetic compass with attachments for the drift indicators.

Stowed in the fuselage is a rubber collapsible boat with a pair of oars. A similar boat was carried by Lindbergh.

CHAPTER XXX

Notable Passages Across the Atlantic

ENTERPRISE, adventure, and daring belong to no one race in particular; they are common to all races. But it is a fact worthy of note that the young American who, in this twentieth century, was the first to fly from New York to Paris, was the son of a Norseman; and the first voyager to cross the Atlantic, back in the eleventh century, was a Norseman.

Leif Ericson, galley - 6 months

The details of Leif Ericsson's voyage are lost in the mists of the past. But it is pretty well authenticated that he sailed in a Norse Viking galley to Vinland (presumed to be the North American mainland), traveling some four thousand miles, at the mercy of wind and wave, and reached the northeast coast of the North American continent in an estimated time of six months. That was in the year 1001.

Nearly five hundred years passed before Columbus opened a new world for settlement. Christopher Columbus, an intrepid Italian who had faith in his venture, sailed on his voyage of discovery in the Spanish caravel *Santa Maria*, accompanied by the *Pinta* and the *Nina*, from Palos, Spain, and reached the

West Indies island
which he named San
Salvador. On the
voyage he covered
4500 miles. He set
sail from Spain
August 3, 1492, and
reached San Sal-
vador October 12,
1492.

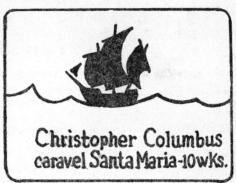

Christopher Columbus
caravel Santa Maria-10wKs.

There followed him, in later years, many sailing
ships of various types, from the *Mayflower*, which
brought the Pilgrims to New England in 1620 (a three-
masted square rigger, only a hundred feet long and
between twenty and twenty-five feet wide), to the
famous American clipper ships of the nineteenth century, some of them 3000 tons gross register, fifteen
times the size of the *Mayflower*.

The third notable voyage was that of Captain Moses
Rogers, commander of the *Savannah*, the first steamship to cross the Atlantic. The *Savannah* was a
combination steam and sail vessel, and left the port
of Savannah, Geor-
gia, bound for Liver-
pool, England, which
it reached in twenty-
nine days and eleven
hours, after a voyage
of about five thou-
sand miles. That
was soon after the
nineteenth century

Moses Rogers, steam-
ship Savannah- 29 days

opened—the year 1819. The *Savannah* was a ship of
350 tons and was built in New York. The vessel was
equipped with sails and side paddles, and used the
paddles on eighteen days of the voyage. Since the
days of the famous *Savannah* the steamship has come
to be a matter of course. The screw propeller displaced the paddle wheels, and steel displaced the
"hearts of oak." To steam and steel has been added
speed, and some idea of how time has been cut in
transatlantic voyages may be gathered from the following records:

The first steamship to cross the Atlantic was the
Savannah, 350 tons, built at New York City, which
left Savannah, Ga., on May 24, 1819, and reached
Liverpool in 29 days, during 18 of which she used
her side paddles. The *Great Western*, on her maiden
voyage from Bristol, England, to New York, covered
the distance in April, 1838, in 15 days. The *Sirius*,
in April, 1838, went from England to New York in
18½ days. The *Britannia*, first Cunard liner, in July,
1840, came from Liverpool to New York in 14 days
8 hours. The *Great Western's* best record across the
ocean was 10 days 10 hours 15 minutes. In May,
1851, the *Pacific* reduced the Atlantic Ocean record
to 9 days 19 hours 25 minutes. The *Persia*, in 1856,
did it in 9 days 1 hour 45 minutes; the *Scotia*, in 1866,
in 8 days 2 hours 48 minutes; the *City of Brussels*, in
1869, in 7 days 22 hours 3 minutes; the *Baltic*, in 1873,
in 7 days 20 hours 9 minutes; the *City of Berlin*, in
1875, in 7 days 15 hours 48 minutes; the *Arizona*,
in 1880, in 7 days 7 hours 23 minutes; the *Alaska*, in
1882, in 6 days 18 hours 37 minutes; the *Etruria*,

in 1888, in 6 days 1 hour 55 minutes; the *Majestic*, in
1891, in 5 days 18 hours 8 minutes; the *Lucania*,
in 1894, in 5 days 7 hours 23 minutes; the *Lusitania*,
in 1908, in 4 days 15 hours; the *Mauretania*, in 1910,
in 4 days 10 hours 41 minutes, at the rate of 26.06
knots an hour.   The foregoing records, since and
including 1856, are between New York and Queens-
town, Ireland.

The best run from New York to Havre was made
by the *France*, of the French line, in 5 days 17 hours.

The most notable passage of the Atlantic by steamship, so far as speed
is concerned, was
that of the *Maure-
tania*, which, under
the command of
Captain David Dow,
covered the distance
between Queens-
town, Ireland, and
Ambrose Light, New

David Dow, steamship
Mauretania - 4 da., 10 hr.

York Harbor, 2780 nautical miles, in 4 days 10 hours
41 minutes.   That was in September, 1910.

First then we have the Viking galley of Ericsson;
then the caravel of Columbus; then the combination
steam-and-sailing ship, *Savannah;* then the great ocean
liner *Mauretania*, with its speed record; a steady development in transatlantic travel that has made the
ocean passage a pleasure.

Then came the era of the submarine, a remarkable
contrivance, but admittedly of little practical use except
in war time.   The first submarine to cross the Atlantic

Paul Koenig, submarine
Deutschland - 16 days

was the *Deutschland*, commanded by Captain Paul Koenig, which made the trip from Bremen, Germany, by way of Heligoland, to Baltimore, Maryland, some 3800 miles, in sixteen days. That was in July, 1916, during the World War.

Then man spurned earth and water, and the next notable passage of the Atlantic is by air line. The year 1919 is especially notable in this respect. The first flying machine to cross the Atlantic was the *NC-4*, a United States Navy seaplane, under command of Lieutenant Commander Read. The first leg of the flight was from Long Island to Newfoundland; then from Newfoundland to Horta and Ponta Delgada in the Azores; and from the Azores to Lisbon, Portugal. That was in May, 1919. Three navy planes, the *NC-1*, *NC-3*, and *N C-4*, started on that first flight, but only one finished, the *NC-4*. The others were so badly damaged when they reached the Azores that they were unable to continue the journey. It should be said that a line of sixty

A·C·Read, seaplane NC-4
26 hours, 41 minutes

AMUNDSEN'S POLAR AIRSHIP "NORGE"

First airship to reach the North Pole.

LINDBERGH, BYRD, AND CHAMBERLIN

Three famous "firsts" in the annals of aviation: Lindbergh, first to fly from New York to Paris; Byrd, first to fly to the North Pole; Chamberlin, first to fly from New York to Germany.

destroyers stretched across the ocean to radio advice to the fliers and give assistance if it were needed.

When the *NC-4* arrived at Lisbon the excitement of the populace was in-

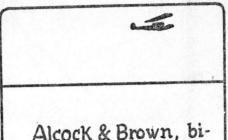

Alcock & Brown, biplane - 16 hr., 12 min.

tense. For the first time in history the vast Atlantic Ocean had been bridged by aircraft, and the indomitable aviators had successfully brought their plane to rest in Portuguese waters after a flight of over two thousand miles from British North America to Europe, via the Azores.

When the birdmen flew into the Portuguese harbor on that 27th of May, 1919, the minds of thoughtful men went back to the days of the early Portuguese pioneers of the Atlantic—to that munificent patron of voyagers and explorers and one of the heroes of modern discovery, Henry, Prince of Portugal, surnamed "The Navigator,"who jovially declared, "The sea is as easy to sail in as the waters at home," who directed the exploration of the unknown seas of the world, and changed the Atlantic "Sea of Dark-

G.H. Scott, dirigible R-34 - 108 hours

ness" into a sea of light; to Vasco, the first navigator who made the voyage to the East Indies by the Cape of Good Hope; to Pedro Alvarez Cabral, who sailed from this same port of Lisbon and, reaching the coast of Brazil in the year 1500, took possession of the territory in the name of Portugal.

And now from that continent on the other side of the Atlantic had come the conquerors of the air, forerunners of a new epoch, as the Portuguese and Spanish navigators had been, four hundred years before.

The flight of the *NC-4*, which had been made in 26 hours 41 minutes, actual flying time, did not end at Lisbon. After covering the 2150 miles between Newfoundland and Portugal, by way of the Azores, the seaplane hopped off for Plymouth, England, the final lap that would complete the transatlantic flight as scheduled.

Here, at Plymouth, on May 31, they were to set foot on the shores of the harbor from which the Pilgrim fathers took ship for a new world three hundred years before. Here, after a flight of 3936 nautical or 4526 statute miles, made in the flying time of 52 hours 31 minutes, congratulations of British and American officials were received.

In the following month, June, 1919, came the next notable passage of the Atlantic—the first nonstop flight from Newfoundland to Ireland. This was made by Captain John Alcock and Lieutenant A. W. Brown, in a British Vickers-Vimy bombing biplane, which flew the 1960 miles between St. John's, Newfoundland, and Clifden, Ireland, in 16 hours 12 minutes. There were no protective destroyers on this trip. These

British eagles soared out over a lonely sea, as Lindbergh did, eight years later, on his flight from New York to Paris.

The first attempt at a nonstop passage across the Atlantic was made by Harry G. Hawker and Lieut. Commander Mackenzie Grieve of the British Royal Navy, who hopped off from St. John's, Newfoundland, in a Sowith biplane on May 18, 1919.

An hour after Hawker and Grieve took off, two other Britishers, Captain Frederick P. Raynham and Captain C. W. F. Morgan, attempted to get away in a Martinsyde biplane, but an axle of the plane broke and the machine was wrecked. Both these attempts and the successful flight made by Alcock and Brown a month later were for a prize of $50,000 offered by the London *Daily Mail*.

Captain Alcock, who was knighted by King George for his exploit, lived only a few months to enjoy his honors. He was killed in December of the same year when his plane crashed at Rouen, France.

For six days after Hawker and Grieve took off there was no word of them. They were given up as lost when suddenly word came from a British warship off the Orkney Islands, near the northern coast of Scotland, that the British fliers were aboard. They had been forced down when 1050 miles from the Newfoundland coast and still 850 miles from Ireland when a water pump choked and disabled the engine.

They were picked up by the Danish steamer, *Mary*, bound from New Orleans to Denmark, and as the *Mary* had no wireless outfit they were unable to inform the world of their safety.

That remarkable year of our Lord 1919 also saw the first transatlantic voyage in a lighter-than-air ship. This achievement was accomplished by Major G. H. Scott, commanding the British dirigible *R-34*. He took off from East Fortune, Edinburgh, and arrived

Hugo EcKener, dirigible ZR-3 (LosAngeles) - 80 hr.

at Mineola, Long Island, N. Y., in 108 hours 12 minutes, flying a distance of 3130 miles. That was in June, 1919. The return voyage by air was also made safely. On the return flight the distance covered was 3200 miles.

The next notable Atlantic passage, also in a lighter-than-air ship, was that of the *ZR-3*, now the United States Navy airship *Los Angeles*. Under command of Dr. Hugo Eckener, this great dirigible left Friedrichshafen, Germany, and was piloted over the Atlantic to Lakehurst, N. J., accomplishing the distance, a little over 5000 miles, in 80 hours 45 minutes, beating all records for flying distance over the Atlantic. That was in October, 1924.

In 1926 Captain Rene Fonck, the famous French war ace, made an attempt to cross the Atlantic in a specially constructed Sikorsky biplane. The plane was on the runway at Roosevelt Field, from which Lindbergh took off on his epoch-making flight, and after a short run overturned and burned. Two of Captain Fonck's crew were killed.

A peculiarly poignant tragedy of the transatlantic air crossing came only a short day or two before Lindbergh hopped off for Paris, when Captain Charles Nungesser and Captain François Coli, compatriots of Captain Fonck and, like him, the possessors of enviable war records, set off from Le Bourget airdrome in Paris in an attempt to reach New York. What happened to the gallant aviators is not known at this writing, and may be forever one of the mysteries of the broad Atlantic.

THE OCEAN FLIERS

Prior to Lindbergh's pioneer flight from New York to Paris, the following is the record of flights over the Atlantic Ocean:

Commander Read, U. S. naval seaplane *NC-4*, Newfoundland to Lisbon via Azores, 2520 miles, May, 1919.

Alcock and Brown, British fliers, Newfoundland to Ireland, 1960 miles, June, 1919.

Commander Scott, British dirigible *R-34*, Scotland to Long Island, 3130 miles, return voyage to England, 3200 miles, June, 1919.

German Zeppelin *ZR-3* (later renamed *Los Angeles*), Friedrichshafen to Lakehurst, N. J., 5006 miles, October, 1924.

Commander Franco, Spanish aviator, Spain to Brazil, February, 1926.

American around-the-world flight, via Scotland, Iceland, Greenland and Labrador, 1924.

François de Pinedo, Africa to Brazil, 1900 miles, February, 1927.

Captain St. Roman, French flier, Africa to Brazil, April, 1927. Still missing.

Nungesser and Coli left Paris for New York, May 8, 1927. Still missing.

To this record may now be added Lindbergh's flight of 3647 miles from New York to Paris, May 20–21, 1927; and the "mystery" flight of Clarence D. Chamberlin, who, with his backer, Charles A. Levine, aboard his plane, hopped off from New York, June 4 (just as Lindbergh was sailing from Cherbourg), and successfully accomplished the ocean hop, landing at Eisleben, about 110 miles southwest of Berlin, at 5 A. M. (German time) June 6 (midnight of June 5, New York time).

CHAPTER XXXI

THE CONQUEST OF THE POLE BY AIR

ANTEDATING Lindbergh's famous flight by just one year was the achievement of Commander Richard Evelyn Byrd, who, accompanied by Floyd Bennett as pilot, made a round-trip flight to the North Pole and back, from Kings Bay, Spitzbergen, on May 9, 1926—the first time in history that an airplane had reached the Pole.

Byrd and Bennett fairly earned the record of being the first fliers to accomplish what Peary and Matt Henson and four Eskimos did with sledge and dogs. But what a difference! Byrd and his Fokker three-motored monoplane did in about fifteen and a half hours what it took Peary over two months to accomplish from base to base! As a matter of fact, Peary was out of touch with civilization for 429 days, and although he discovered the Pole on April 6, 1909, it was not until five months later that he was able to flash a message from Labrador. Commander Byrd and his pilot were away from civilization for less than sixteen hours, and considering that they carried wireless transmitting sets, they were not out of touch with civilization at any time.

This is an indication of how great has been the advance in travel and communication. When Lindbergh hopped off from Roosevelt Field all the world knew of it, and when he landed at Paris not only the story of his lone flight was flashed around the globe, but the photographs taken by the Paris camera men were radioed across the Atlantic and reproduced in American newspapers within a few hours. So far have we traveled from Peary's day!

THAT EVENTFUL APRIL 6TH

Peary reached the Pole on April 6th, and it was on the same day, seventeen years later, that Commander Byrd left New York on the Shipping Board steamer *Chantier*, bound for Spitzbergen and the North Pole. He took with him two airplanes—a Fokker three-engined machine equipped with Wright 200-horsepower engines, and a Curtiss auxiliary single-engined plane.

Soon after his arrival at Spitzbergen, the engines of the Fokker plane—named the *Josephine Ford*, for a little daughter of Edsel Ford, one of the financial backers—were "warmed up," and on May 5 Pilot Bennett made his initial trial hop, a flight of two hours.

May 9, 1926, was the eventful day. On that day the dash to the Pole and back was accomplished in fifteen hours and fifty-one minutes.

The fliers were favored by continuous sunlight, and there was never the slightest fog, enabling Commander Byrd to use his sun compass and bubble sextant and obtain the most accurate observations possible.

Bennett and Byrd alternated in the piloting, Bennett refilling the gasoline containers while the Commander piloted and navigated.

They saw no sign of life of any kind after entering the ice pack. No birds, seals, polar bears, nor traces of them were seen.

They arrived at the Pole at 9.04 A. M. Greenwich

COMMANDER RICHARD BYRD AND THE FOKKER NORTH POLE PLANE

This was the first airplane to fly over the North Pole, May 9, 1926.

Photo *Underwood & Underwood, N. Y.*

COMMANDER JOHN RODGERS AND THE PN9 No. 1

The giant seaplane with its Commander, which flew to Hawaii on August 31, 1925. The plane

time, when the sun was about 33 degrees from their line of flight, which, while not the best possible position, was very good.

When Commander Byrd knew by the time he had been flying that he should be approaching the Pole, he measured the sun's altitude with the bubble sextant. The readings became smaller and smaller as he went along, and when they reached the value that he had tabulated for the Pole for the particular time, he knew he was there.

The fact that he was able to turn about and retrace his steps, so to speak, without a single landmark, and after being in the air over fifteen hours, was in itself a spectacular example of accurate navigation.

THE FLIGHT OF THE "NORGE"

A few days later the great airship *Norge*, of the Amundsen-Ellsworth-Nobile expedition, soared outward from Kings Bay, on the trail to the Pole blazed by Byrd and Bennett, and continued on over the top of the world to Alaska.

It was on May 11, 1926, that the *Norge* started out on her voyage of over 2000 miles from Kings Bay, Spitzbergen, to Point Barrow, Alaska, and thence 600 miles farther to Nome.

The North Pole was reached at 1.30 on the morning of May 12.

About five hours later the so-called "Ice Pole," or "Pole of Inaccessibility," was reached. After passing through fogs and flying bits of ice, the Alaska coast was sighted, and a safe landing was made at Teller, on May 14, after a flight of 71 hours. The actual distance flown by the *Norge*, as reckoned by the pilot, was 3291 miles.

The *Norge* was a semi-rigid airship, 347 feet in length, with a gas capacity of 640,000 cubic feet. It was designed and built for the Italian government by Colonel Umberto Nobile, who commanded the airship on its flight over the Pole. It was purchased for the Amundsen-Ellsworth-Nobile Expedition and piloted by easy stages from Rome to Spitzbergen, where it took off for Alaska.

In the great exploit Captain Roald Amundsen, Norway's hero and the discoverer of the South Pole (December 14, 1911), shared laurels with Colonel Nobile, Italian commander, and builder of the *Norge*, and with Lincoln Ellsworth, American, one of the leaders of the expedition from first to last.

CHAPTER XXXII

THE EAGLE'S RETURN TO THE HOMELAND

IT was well for Lindbergh that a week's solid rest came to him upon the *Memphis*. It was well for him that his stores of vitality that had been exhausted by the series of receptions and flights in Europe had been restocked. America was waiting full-handed, full-hearted, and full-throated to give him such a welcome as no man has received in recent years.

While he was homeward bound Governor Sam A. Baker, of Missouri, issued a commission promoting him from a captaincy to colonel in the Missouri National Guards. The commission was made effective May 21, the day he landed in Paris after his transatlantic flight. That commission entitled him to wear the spread eagles which are the emblems of his new rank and which most fitly serve to remind the world of his epochal flight.

The long days on the ocean were almost devoid of incident. He made friends with the ship's mascot, a kangaroo which loved to nibble at the flowers in his cabin. He ate on successive days in the various messes, so that when the *Memphis* came to its berth in Washington he had dined or supped with everybody aboard from the cabin boy to commander.

From sky and sea and land, on Saturday, June 13, America roared and waved its welcome to the youngest and latest of its heroes, Colonel Charles Augustus Lindbergh, the Lone Eagle.

Never has conqueror or emperor received so thunderous and universal an acclaim. Fresh from the honors of adoring France, mighty England, and grateful Belgium, this most modest and most daring of men came to his own land to find his personal traits set up as new national ideals.

He found awaiting him the President of his country as the head of all the American people, and at the President's side, his own mother, with starry, tearmisted eyes.

At the gangplank, he found throngs of aviators, each wearing the spread eagle showing active, death-daring service.

The streets of the Capital were banked from curb to house line with cheering hundreds of thousands and above them floated his flag in endless rippling waves.

Through that multitude rode a youth of twenty-five upon whose fresh, tanned face amazement was still marked. The naïveté that had caused him to bring six letters of introduction to Paris and had phrased "I am Charles A. Lindbergh" as his first words in France, was still to be read in the slightly puzzled look he turned upon the fairyland all around him.

"Surely," said that expression, "this is not altogether for me. There must be something for which I am a symbol that brings these people together."

All through the long day that expression lasted. When he walked among his fellow Minnesotans, when he spoke briefly and modestly with Hoover and Kellogg and the other members of the Cabinet, when he sat at dinner with the President, Mrs. Coolidge, and his mother, he seemed to be wanting to rub his eyes in an effort to awaken.

Something of this feeling was in his words throughout the welcoming ceremonies. Once in a while he said, "I am not worthy of all this fuss."

Always, he acknowledged the tumult and the outpouring of greetings as something with which he was connected only impersonally. It was as though he were standing alone upon some eminence watching a mighty recessional to some hero of another world.

PANORAMA OF PATRIOTISM

The early hours of his golden day were passed amid a panorama of patriotism and beauty. As his homeward-bound ship, the cruiser *Memphis*, slowly passed Mount Vernon, a ruffle of drums sounded from the shore.

The flag was run up to full mast over the home where the Father of His Country had lived and died. Silvery bugles called the strains of "The Star-Spangled Banner" across the velvet lawns while Lindbergh, deeply stirred, stood upon the bridge of the ship.

Overhead, more than a hundred planes of all classes, led by the *Los Angeles*, mightiest of dirigibles, convoyed the Eagle on his way.

All along the trip up the Potomac a chorus of whistles and cannonading told of the ship's advance. Every clearing had its cluster of flags and groups of cheering men, women, and children.

It was at the Washington Navy Yard that the first great thrill of the day came to the flier. He was standing upon the bridge peering into the throng around the

dock with those marvelous eyes of his that have double
the normal power of vision.   Suddenly he straightened
as a pointer stiffens when he scents a bird.   Again he
bent forward, eyes intent and focused.

A word to an officer at his side, and powerful marine
glasses were in his hand.   Excitedly he trained them
where his unaided eyes had seen a form he thought
he recognized.   Sure enough, there she was, the mother
to whom he had telephoned from Paris the morning
after he had flown across the Atlantic.

She was not in the front line.   Surrounded by
hundreds, she would have been missed by any other
mortal eyes.   Eager hands brought a box, lifted her
on it, and watched her with streaming eyes as she
waved a damp handkerchief to her adored son.

Skies clear, calm, and smiling made a blue and white
canopy for the most vivid, inspiring, and patriotic
scene the Capital had ever witnessed over the wide
expanse of the campus in which is the huge obelisk to
Washington, the Father of His Country.   Aircraft
droned ceaselessly; squadrons of bombers, scouts,
and pursuit planes in battle formation zoomed and
snored from 11 o'clock until the arrival of the President.

The *Los Angeles* was like an immense silver fish
swimming in a surf of high clouds and was attended by
a mosquito swarm of pursuit ships.

The crowd came upon the sunswept plateau early,
taking their chances of sunstroke in the tropic heat.
Tens of thousands of sensible ones remained in the cool
shelter of the trees surrounding the monument grounds.
Boy Scouts, many coming "Lindberghs" in their rank,
aided the police and soldiers in holding the lines along

the streets and in the Potomac Park. Until a half hour before the parade arrived carpenters and decorators were at work on the imposing temporary stands where the President and the Nation's guest spoke. It was a dignified temple of white pillars topped at the peaks by radiant new flags. Along both wings of the big platform telegraphers chattered like magpies at their keys.

Beneath the platform radio-control stations and the equipment for the big amplifiers were installed, with experts at the switches.

WHILE ALL AMERICA LISTENED IN

Broadcasters told the story of the oncoming procession from the upper deck of the President's stand, and one announcer located strategically at the very top of the Washington Monument broadcast his description of the scene to a waiting world.

Hundreds of newspaper correspondents were in the section assigned to them on both sides of the pavilion. Foreign tongues poured and clashed in these rows of journalists—Spanish, Japanese, French, German, Scandinavian, Polish, and Russian in the native idioms were heard.

Every diplomatic colony was in the stand of honor. Senators and their families, Congressmen, Cabinet Ministers, high army and navy officers, touched elbows as the procession approached them.

Ready to record for posterity every phase of the historic ceremony, the largest number of movie and still photographers adjusted their cameras. Their vantage point was a high, raised platform immediately facing the Presidential daïs. In a white loft near the base of the Washington Monument, forty-eight homing pigeons, one for each state, awaited the springing of their trap doors.

And now the announcer sent through the amplifiers the story of Lindbergh's approach. He was upon the gangplank, his brother aviators were greeting him. He had taken his place at the head of the line with members of the Cabinet and some of the highest personages in the land as his escort of honor. He had come to the historic east plaza of the Capitol where Presidents are inaugurated and kings of other lands received. The cavalry and the bands are ready, the triumphal parade down Pennsylvania Avenue has commenced, the crowds are cheering and Lindbergh flushed brighter and happier as he bows to right and left. As the crowd in the monument grounds listened, the heat grew more intense. Two women have fainted, the Boy Scouts rush buckets of ice water to their relief, they are taken to Red Cross stations on the grounds.

The broadcaster announces that the President has left the temporary White House at du Pont Circle for the stands. Thousands emerged from the shaded safety of the trees to press closely against the ropes in the green broiler that is the monument plateau. Everything was ready for the ceremony of bestowing upon the youngest colonel in the United States the first flying cross provided by Congress for distinguished service in the air.

The policing here was so well organized that the throng was handled skilfully and easily. It was demonstrated as the surge of humanity beat against the ropes

48 HOME COMERS!
One for every State

COLONEL LINDBERGH ADDRESSES THE AMERICAN PEOPLE

Speaking over the radio at the Washington Monument. At the left President Coolidge, who has just decorated him with the Distinguished Flying Cross, is applauding the speech.

LINDBERGH DECORATED IN SHADOW OF THE
WASHINGTON MONUMENT

In an impressing ceremony held at the foot of America's tribute to her first President, Colonel Lindbergh was decorated by President Coolidge with the highest honor known to aviation, the Distinguished Flying Cross.

and was held by that barrier, that Washington was the place most fit to receive Lindbergh; in any other city the wave of welcome would have swept aside all resistance.

APPROACH OF THE PRESIDENT

And now the President approached, preceded by long lines of stately motors bearing the last rush of diplomats, Senators, and high dignitaries.

Music of a half dozen bands swept over Potomac Park, foretelling the approach of Lindbergh. The President's own troop of cavalry was in the van as the stately procession swept through the avenue of trees. Three superb negro troopers were in the first line, sitting on their steeds like statues of carved ebony. A squadron of mounted artillery with galloping mules swept across, and directly back of them came the President's motor.

The President and Mrs. Coolidge received a tremendous ovation from the immense and highly wrought crowd. They stepped to the front of the daïs and after a fanfare of golden trumpets the Marine Band swung into the thrilling strains of "The Star-Spangled Banner."

As the strain ended the President and Mrs. Coolidge stepped back into their box, the only bit of shade in the wide sunswept expanse. Secretary of the Treasury Mellon sat directly back of the President and beside him were Attorney General Sargent and Secretary of State Kellogg. Secret Service operators, under the general direction of "Dick" Jervis, stationed themselves at the corners of the stands and upon the fringes of the crowd.

Mrs. Woodrow Wilson entered the stand, immediately following the President, and was assigned a seat of honor beside the President's box. The usual bustle of anticipation and exchange of greetings filled in the few moments of waiting while Lindbergh and his escort approached.

The line of infantry that guarded the approach of the stand stood with fixed bayonets, a usual precaution against a sudden rush.

A red and white guidon of the cavalry escort rode like a gay bird on the crest of the cheers as the procession wound its way to the platform. The lines of infantry presented arms. Suddenly one of them in khaki emitted a low sigh, his legs crumpled and he slid slowly to earth, using his bayoneted rifle as a staff which failed to stay his fall. The terrific heat had sapped his vitality. Boy Scouts and officers who were not in the infantry line picked him up and bore him unconscious to the Red Cross station.

The cheering cracked like steady, sharp rifle fire as Lindbergh and his mother came through the banks of humanity to the President's stand. He wore the double-breasted blue serge suit he had bought in Paris the Monday after his arrival there. The soft felt hat, with wide black band that also came from Paris, was in his lap.

The healthy coat of tan which his young face had acquired in California during the days when he was testing the *Spirit of St. Louis* was still upon him. The keen, blue eyes that had been handed down by his Scandinavian and Irish forebears were clouded by the mist of strong emotion. His right hand held his hat and his left hand was gripped by both hands of his mother.

MOTHER AND SON

His sole expression was that of youth shy, yet daring, who had been awakened after a sound sleep to find the world at his feet. Amazement still struggled with joy. From time to time he turned to his mother as she said something of interest to him.

The face of that mother should have been reproduced in imperishable pigment, that all the world of sons yet to be born might see what happiness might come from their achievement. It shone with sublime and perfect happiness, a happiness too deep and sacred for words. Her dress of light silk, suitable for the terrific heat, set off her matronly dignity most beautifully.

As Lindbergh advanced to the stands a tumult of tremendous cheering went up. It swept on and on in pulsing waves that renewed themselves as they were about to come to an end. The roar drowned the song of the bugles and the booming of the drums.

It subsided only when the President stepped to the front of the stands to welcome Lindbergh. The President's speech was punctuated by bursts of cheering as he told of America's pride in Lindbergh. Never did Mr. Coolidge express more enthusiasm than when he greeted the Lone Eagle's heroic feat on behalf of the American people.

THE PRESIDENT'S SPEECH

"My fellow countrymen," he began: "It was in America that the modern art of flying of heavier-than-air machines was first developed. As the experiments became successful, the airplane was devoted to practical purposes. It has been adapted to commerce in the transportation of passengers and mail and used for national defense by our land and sea forces. Beginning with a limited flying radius, its length has been gradually extended.

"We have made flying records. Our army fliers have circumnavigated the globe. One of our navy men started from California and flew far enough to have reached Hawaii, but being off his course landed in the water. Another officer of the navy has flown to the North Pole. Our own country has been traversed from shore to shore in a single flight.

"It had been apparent for some time that the next great feat in the air would be a continuous flight from the mainland of America to the mainland of Europe. Two courageous Frenchmen made the reverse attempt and passed to a fate that is as yet unknown. Others were speeding their preparations to make the trial, but it remained for an unknown youth to tempt the elements and win. It is the same story of valor and victory by a son of the people that shines through every page of American history.

"Twenty-five years ago there was born in Detroit, Mich., a boy, representing the best traditions of this country, of a stock known for its deeds of adventure and exploration. His father, moved with a desire for public service, was a member of Congress for several terms. His mother, who dowered her son with her own modesty and charm, is with us today. Engaged in the vital profession of school-teaching, she has permitted neither money nor fame to interfere with her fidelity to her duties.

"Too young to have enlisted in the World War, her son became a student at one of the big State universities. His interest in aviation led him to an army aviation school; and in 1925 he was graduated as an airplane pilot. In November, 1926, he had reached the rank of captain in the Officers' Reserve Corps. Making his home in St. Louis, he had joined the 110th Observation Squadron of the Missouri National Guard.

THE LONE EAGLE'S ADMIRABLE QUALITIES

"Some of his qualities noted by the army officers who examined him for promotion, as shown by reports in the files of the Militia Bureau of the War Department, are as follows: 'Intelligent,' 'industrious,' 'energetic,' 'dependable,' 'purposeful,' 'alert,' 'quick of action,' 'serious,' 'deliberate,' 'stable,' 'efficient,' 'frank,' 'modest,' 'congenial,' 'a man of good moral habits and regular in all his business transactions.' One of the officers expressed his belief that the young man 'would successfully complete everything he undertakes.' This reads like a prophecy.

"Later he became connected with the United States mail service, where he exhibited marked ability and from which he is now on leave of absence.

"On a morning just three weeks ago yesterday this wholesome, earnest, fearless, courageous product of America rose into the air from Long Island in a monoplane christened the *Spirit of St. Louis*, in honor of his home and that of his supporters. It was no haphazard adventure.

INSPIRED BY VIKING BLOOD

"After months of most careful preparation, supported by a valiant character, driven by an unconquerable will, and inspired by the imagination and the spirit of his Viking ancestors, this reserve officer set wing across the dangerous stretches of the North Atlantic. He was alone. His destination was Paris.

"Thirty-three hours and thirty minutes later, in the evening of the second day, he landed at his destination on the French flying field at Le Bourget. He had traveled over 3600 miles and established a new and remarkable record. The execution of his project was a perfect exhibition of art.

"This country will always remember the way in which he was received by the people of France, by their President and by their Government. It was the more remarkable because they were mourning the disappearance of their intrepid countrymen, who had tried to span the Atlantic on a western flight.

"Our messenger of peace and good will had broken down another barrier of time and space and brought two great peoples into closer communion. In less than a day and a half he had crossed the ocean over which Columbus had traveled for sixty-nine days and the Pilgrim Fathers for sixty-six days on their way to the New World.

"But, above all, in showering applause and honor upon this genial, modest, American youth, with the naturalness, the simplicity and the poise of true greatness, France had the opportunity to show clearly her good will for America and our people. With like acclaim and evidences of cordial friendship our Ambassador without portfolio was received by the rulers, the Governments, and the peoples of England and Belgium. From other nations came hearty messages of admiration for him and for his country. For these manifold evidences of friendship we are profoundly grateful.

THE LONE EAGLE'S SILENT PARTNER

"The absence of self-acclaim, the refusal to become commercialized, which has marked the conduct of this sincere and genuine exemplar of fine and noble virtues, has endeared him to everyone. He has returned unspoiled. Particularly has it been delightful to have him refer to his airplane as somehow possessing a personality and being equally entitled to credit with himself, for we are proud that in every particular this silent partner represented American genius and industry. I am told that more than one hundred separate companies furnished materials, parts, or service in its construction.

"And now, my fellow citizens, this young man has returned. He is here. He has brought his unsullied fame home. It is our great privilege to welcome him back to his native land, on behalf of his own people, who have a deep affection for him, and have been thrilled by his splendid achievement, a colonel of our Republic, a conqueror of the air and strengthener of the ties which bind us to our sister nations across the sea, and, as President of the United States, I bestow the distinguished flying cross as symbol of appreciation for what he is and what he has done, upon Colonel Charles A. Lindbergh."

FACING THE AMERICAN THOUSANDS

At the close of the President's speech Lindbergh stepped to the edge of the stand as the cheering broke all past records. He had the ease born of talks with kings; no nervousness was noticeable and his voice was in his ordinary tone. Practice had told him how to face the microphone; the multitudes of Le Bourget and Brussels and Croydon had prepared him for the American thousands upon thousands in Washington. Bravely, briefly, deliberately, and clearly he said:

"On the evening of the 21st of May, last, I arrived at Le Bourget, Paris. During the week I spent in France, the day in Belgium, and the short period in London and England, the people of France and the people of Europe requested that I bring back to the people of America one message from the people of France and the people of Europe. At every gathering, at every meeting I attended, were the same words, 'You have seen the affection of the people of France and the people of Europe for the people of America demonstrated to you—"

Here the speech was broken by a thundering moment of applause. Then Lindbergh continued his quotation of the message he declared had been sent back to America from Europe, saying:

" 'Demonstrated to you. Upon your return to your country take back with you this message from France and Europe to the United States of America.'

"I thank you."

As he finished he leaned far over the railing of the rostrum. The crowd was silent for fully a minute;

THE LINDBERGHS AT THE WHITE HOUSE

Colonel Lindbergh and his mother were the house guests of
President and Mrs. Coolidge. The group is seen on the steps of
the temporary White House on Du Pont Circle.

THE LIVING HERO OF THE AIR PAYING HOMAGE TO THE HERO DEAD

Colonel Lindbergh is seen placing a wreath on the tomb of the Unknown Soldier in Arlington Cemetery, Washington, while the Military Guard of Honor salutes.

plainly it was taken by surprise at the brevity of Lindbergh.

SPARING OF SPEECH

What he said and the way he said it were true to his character. He had been sparing of speech, modest of demeanor before the royalties and multitudes of Europe. He was no less brief and modest now. The President and Mrs. Coolidge, who had shaken hands with him formally when he came upon the platform, now shook hands with him again by way of congratulation for his perfect reply to the welcome of all Americans.

The first flying cross ever conferred upon an American had been pinned upon the blue coat of Lindbergh by the President. It came to the youngest colonel in American history and generals and admirals, who had won their honors in action, were there to do him honor.

Before him, the largest battery of motion and still cameras ever assembled whirred and clicked while forty-eight homing pigeons, one from every state in the Union, flew like feathered bullets to all points of the compass bearing the news.

The heat upon that unsheltered terrain was terrific and a number of prostrated men and women were treated in the tents of the Red Cross, but the throng seemed to mind the heat and other discomforts not at all. They came to see and to hear Lindbergh and they were satisfied.

As they left the stands—the President and the youth who had won renown in a few short weeks—the crowd pressed more closely and insistently against the ropes.

The soldiers with their bayoneted rifles pressed back the waves.

The cavalry again swung into line and Lindbergh left the torrid field, his left hand pressed tightly between the hands of his mother.

MOTHER REFUSES TO SHARE GLORY

The famous crooked smile of Lindbergh with its flash of gleaming was working overtime as the motor made its way slowly to the temporary White House. Right and left he bowed, cannon barked a thundering succession of welcomes and bands blared along the triumphal way, while Lindbergh acknowledged the cheers and calls of the crowd by bows to right and left.

The eyes of his mother looked only into his or straight ahead. She had said that all the glory was for him and she would not distract from it. Shouts of "Hurrah for Mrs. Lindbergh" went unnoticed. Once in a while her son called her attention to them, but she shook her head smilingly. This was his day and she would only sit by, remembering the joy that would have come to the father they both had loved.

The return trip to the temporary White House on du Pont Circle merged into the family nature again. Issuing forth in official order, eighteen cars bearing the high Cabinet members and others as attendants, three cars sufficed to bring back President and Mrs. Coolidge, Colonel Lindbergh and his mother, and the White House aides.

At 1.37 o'clock the hospitable doors of the mansion were opened, and the group was swallowed up, the only hint of the high adventure which had led to the precedent honors being a small plaster model of the *Spirit of St. Louis*, in the entrance hall.   Mrs. Lindbergh had borne up remarkably well through the extreme test that had been placed on the pride of motherhood in all that had gone before. The same sweet smile flashed a farewell to the surrounding crowds as the door closed upon her.

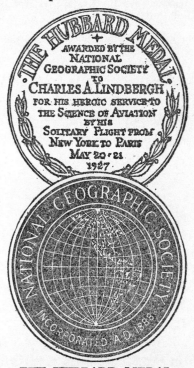

Luncheon followed almost immediately on the arrival at the Patterson mansion.   Later came the ovation by Colonel Lindbergh's native state, at the meeting of the Minnesota Society at the New Willard Hotel, with Secretary of State Kellogg making the welcoming address.   There was presented the Memorial Volume, the official papers and correspondence that had signalized

THE HUBBARD MEDAL
Presented to Colonel Lindbergh by the National Geographic Society.

the progress of Colonel Lindbergh's record-breaking feat.

The long, eventful day closed with a reception by the National Press Club.

Here the Lone Eagle met informally men of his own age who hailed him as the pioneer of a better day.

Here he was eulogized and again modestly disavowed the need for so much glorification.

AN INTIMATE VIEW OF LINDBERGH

From Mr. Charles F. Traung, Commissioner of Athletics, California, who journeyed all the way to Washington to be present at the official reception of the Flying Viking, we have this colorful picture of the scene on the Potomac:

"Through the courtesy of Secretary of the Navy Wilbur, my brother and I received official passes on the escort boat *Porpoise*, which also carried representatives of the ·press. We proceeded down the Potomac River about ten miles and met the cruiser *Memphis*, steaming at her side until the Navy Yard was reached.

"It was a grand sight and one long to be remembered: Coming up the river with at least seventy-five aëroplanes overhead doing all kinds of wild stunts, and in contrast the airship *Los Angeles* sailing gracefully over the cruiser. Pleasure craft of all sizes, decorated in glaring colors, plying back and forth outside the patrol limits; the shores of the beautiful Potomac lined for miles on both sides with people, doing homage to this typical American youth who was unheard of a month ago.

"An incident occurred on the *Porpoise* that showed what this tousled-haired boy thinks of his country. When our boat pulled close to the *Memphis*, Lindbergh was standing on the bridge with some of the officers. When the women on the old *Porpoise*, as if the inspiration struck them all at the same time, burst out in rich and clear tones and sang "America"; and when the strains of the old hymn died away this splendid boy (for boy he is) saluted, and we could see him turn and brush aside a tear.

"There were many of us that felt a tightness in our throats and pride in our hearts that this fine, clean-cut, unspoiled youth was an American.

"And after the boats docked, and his mother, accompanied by one of the ship officers, ascended the gangplank to meet him, he went into one of the cabins, so he could be alone with her. What foresight! To have his mother alone for a few short moments from the madding crowd. And how patiently the crowd waited for them to reappear. Tense moments.

"And then they reappeared: that big, smiling, bashful boy and his proud mother, willing to give themselves over to the crowds that wanted to get a glimpse of this ideal of American boyhood. What an inspiration he will be for this and the next generation!

"We have champions in different sports, and who can deny that he took a sporting chance? He is the champion of all champions. A true athlete, trained to the second, ready for the grand test. And he came through with honor and glory because he was prepared.

"Seeing what we did at Washington, I am doubly sure that this great country knows how to acknowledge and receive one of its own who has added fame and glory to the greatest nation of the world—the good old U. S. A."

AT THE END OF THE DAY

Emotion took its toll from the youthful frame, steel-ribbed though it is. At the end of the day he was dog tired, probably far more weary than he had been at the end of his long flight over the Atlantic.

17

Rest came to him shortly before midnight in the home of the plain New Englander to whom "early to bed" has been a lifelong maxim. The golden day had come to an end.

Not in generations has such emotion swayed Washington as on that day in June when the nation did honor to Lindbergh and the *Spirit of St. Louis*. Wealth and high honors for once passed into the rear and the plain young man of the people was king for a day.

In the rolls of Senators and Congressmen upon the stand were members of the old guard who remembered "Lindy" when he and his dauntless progressive father walked the streets of Washington. They remembered the freckled-faced, sandy-haired lad who went to a Washington school. They had listened to his father's fierce thrusts against wealth and political power. Remembering these things, they saw a likeness to him in the man that flew the *Spirit of St. Louis*.

How deeply that official greeting of Washington touched Lindbergh and his mother cannot be set down in words. For him and her it was a golden day, set apart in imperishable memory; for America, it was a day of high aspirations and new hope. The honors that came to Lindbergh were tributes to an individual human being, to an American who feared not to fare forth into perilous adventures.

As the great throng left the monument ground, only one opinion was heard—Lindbergh was exactly what everyone had expected him to be. He was a radiant sun of the morning. He was the personification of modesty and of superb efficiency. He was the best type of American. He was a greatly loving son.

CHAPTER XXXIII

THE SECOND DAY IN WASHINGTON

PUBLIC prayer, an exhortation to Americans to remember soldiers whose limbs and lives were wrecked by war, silent meditation at the tomb of the Unknown Soldier—these were the patriotic and reverent words and deeds of Colonel Charles A. Lindbergh on his first Sabbath in America since his triumphant return from his now historic transatlantic flight.

All Washington, both official and lay, sweltering under a terrific sun, watched the youthful flier as he motored from the temporary White House in du Pont Circle with his mother and President and Mrs. Coolidge to divine service of First Congregational Church in the Metropolitan Theater, Tenth and F Streets, and back to the President's home. Then he and a military escort went to beautiful Arlington on the hill overlooking the Potomac and thence to Walter Reed Hospital, where he made his only talk of the day and shook hands with scores of hopelessly invalided soldiers of the World War.

Tens of thousands cheered him along the route and called as they applauded his mother, who rode beside him.

It was an exhausting day for both, but they endured it all smilingly and when night came rested serenely and in homelike fashion with the Coolidges, to whom they are already as old friends.

ATTENTIVE DURING SERVICE

To no one has Lindbergh as yet made any statement concerning his religious belief. In Europe, when he attended the services of any church his demeanor was reverential, but he did not appear to be a participant.

In the morning Congregationalist service in the theater that served as temporary quarters, his lips moved and his voice came low and clear as he joined in the recital of the Lord's Prayer. He stood beside President Coolidge in the Presidential pew and like the President read the words of the hymns, but did not participate in the congregational singing.

Attentively he listened while Rev. Jason Noble Pierce prayed for divine guidance for "our chief magistrate and his guest," and later when the clergyman preached from the text, "The words that I speak." Serene, attentive, he still seemed to let his thought wander up to the clouds as he looked through an open window at blue sky and high, gray patches of drifting mist.

While the men in the pew were mute during the singing Mrs. Coolidge and Mrs. Lindbergh sang every note of every hymn. Mrs. Lindbergh's rich contralto surprised by its richness and depth. It was an excellent foil to the light soprano of Mrs. Coolidge.

TALKS WITH WOUNDED VETERANS

The trip to the National Cemetery at Arlington was in keeping with the practice commenced by Colonel Lindbergh in Paris when he placed a wreath upon the tomb of the French Unknown Soldier and later paid

similar tributes to the graves of the Unknown Soldiers
of England and Belgium.

His wreath for the tomb of the man who in death is
as alone as was Lindbergh over the Atlantic was of bay
leaves in which were intertwined red and white carna-
tions and huge red cannas. While thousands waited
he stood before the tomb uncovered and with bowed
head, a silent and statuesque exemplar of patriotism
and grateful memory.

But it was among the poor, bedridden and pain-
racked men of Walter Reed Hospital that he touched
the heights and became patriotically and reverentially
vocal. The contrast between his own unfettered body
and the spirit, less bound by time and place than
any man who has ever been born, and those of soldiers,
many as brave as he, doomed forever to a bed or wheel
chair, brought to him a sudden realization of the
burdens that war have placed upon the shoulders of
mankind.

Here he talked pityingly with shell-shocked and
cruelly wounded aviators, doughboys without arms
and without legs, men almost as young as himself for
whom normal life has ended and who are living upon
the reserves of their courage.

HERO HAILS GREATER HEROES

Out of that deep well of pity, he drew his exhortation to the people of America to remember always and
to care for these victims of battles that were not of
their seeking, of a war into which they put all that life
can hold of happiness and health.

In that brief talk to these shattered men he also

hailed as greater heroes than himself or any other peace-time worker these aviators whose deeds in battle were overshadowed by the welter of carnage and battle all around them. That tribute came as an example of the modesty that distinguished him above all other heroes of our time.

Here, as at the church service and at Arlington, his mother received almost as much attention as he did. At Arlington a sudden rush of women, most of them young, broke through the lines of restraining soldiers to pluck at his sleeves and cry, "Hurrah for Lindy," to his plain embarrassment. During the ceremonies in the amphitheater at Walter Reed Hospital, a man interrupted repeatedly with calls of "Mother, Mother Lindbergh, the best mother in the world. Hurrah for Mrs. Lindbergh!"

INSPECTS REASSEMBLED PLANE

After his emotional visit with the wounded in the hospital he expressed a desire to see what sort of job the mechanics had made of the reassembling of the *Spirit of St. Louis.* The White House motor and its comet-like tail of escorting automobiles sped to Anacostia and thence to Haines Point, where his plane, as good as new, was ready for him on a barge. He inspected it carefully, going over with the men who had worked upon it what they found in the reassembling. Everything was satisfactory and he thanked the men warmly.

He then was driven to Bolling Field, where a group of army aviators awaited him. He climbed into an army pursuit plane, worked the controls, and was photographed with some of his brother fliers. Attendance upon vesper service that was held on the terrace of the Capitol brought the Sabbath to a close. It ended for him as it had commenced, upon a note of reverence.

For them both, this American mother and her son, the day was a happy one, principally because they were together. They seemed to mind the tropic sun not at all as they talked continually to each other on the long motor trips from place to place. The cheering and the honors by now have become a story that has been often told. But their pride and love for each other has deepened and strengthened because he has come back safe from the death that rode beside him in the winds and that waited for him in the waves.

BUGLES ANNOUNCE HIS COMING

Stout ropes and cordons of soldiers kept within bounds the multitude that thronged the beautiful grounds of Walter Reed Hospital to see and hear Lindbergh. A ruse to circumvent other tens of thousands was resorted to by the committee on arrangements when the flier's visit was set ahead an hour. It was three o'clock, instead of the scheduled four o'clock, when a grouping of fifty brilliant flags on the bandstand of the open-air amphitheater announced his approach. Almost immediately bugles at the western entrance of the gate called their warning and the long line of motor cycles and motors whirled up to the main buildings of the great institution.

The hospital is reserved exclusively for soldiers and sailors. Here are assembled for study, treatment, and in many cases, for tender care until death shall relieve the agonies, the most pitiable cases that came to America as human wreckage from the World War.

Colonel Lindbergh and his mother, with John Hays Hammond, who rode with them in the White House motor, were met at the foot of the steps of the main building by Brigadier General J. M. Kennedy, of the medical section of the United States Army, and Brigadier General Amos Fries, commanding the chemical warfare section.

Lindbergh had said he wanted to talk to some of the shell-shocked and bedridden aviators who had been shot down during the war. These and the other hopelessly bedridden cases are on the second floor of the main building and he was taken there immediately by General Kennedy.

By his wish, that part of his visit was not made public. Newspaper men and all other visitors were asked to remain on the ground floor until he returned. It was said later he had passed quickly from bed to bed, giving a warm handclasp here, saying a few words of sympathy and encouragement there to the poor fellows upon whom the door of life has been almost closed.

To everyone on this floor his coming was a great joy. He was their idol, the lad who, like them, had greatly dared.

They did not envy the glory that had come to him while they had been broken on the wheel of fate. Instead, they saw in him the triumph of the soul of man over fears of injury and death. That courage of his gave to them, by mere contact with his brave presence, a joy and a new store of resolution to meet whatever might lie before them.

It was in the open-air amphitheater, however, where the wheel-chair cases were assembled around the speaker's stand, and the legless, armless, and otherwise crippled were aided to seats by nurses, that he showed his greatest interest.

Twenty-four of the most seriously wounded had been waiting for him in the shadeless arena for more than half an hour before he appeared. Behind these and other cripples tens of thousands of sightseers sweltered in the intense sunshine.

PHILADELPHIA VETERAN IN HIGH SPIRIT

None of the wheel-chair cases was more jaunty, more casual, than John L. Connor, of Philadelphia. "I got bumped in France," he explained, "and my heart is leaking all the time. My left side is hopelessly paralyzed and will be as long as I live. I want to see that Lindy lad. He sure has us all skinned for courage."

He would talk but little of his war record. "I was in the 107th Infantry of the Twenty-seventh Division," he said. "O'Ryan was our commander and he was a pip. I was working in New York and joined up over there. That was how I came to be in the Twenty-seventh instead of the Twenty-eighth, where I really belonged."

PRESENTED WITH SCROLL

Nurses noted the growing pallor of Connor and his fellows in the wheel chairs. The sun was burning the vitality out of them as a flame burns down a candle. A hurry call went out for parasols and these quickly came from women in the crowd outside the ropes.

A shout from the hilltop announced that Lindbergh and the others had left the main building and were coming down the grassy slope. They walked through an avenue of cheering thousands. Hands of women and children went out to touch him and his mother as they passed smiling on their way to the stand.

There, after the applause and the cries had subsided, General Fries presented to Lindbergh a basket of flowers sent by veterans of foreign wars coming from Pennsylvania and introduced briefly a "flaming youth of other days," General John L. Clem, commander of the G. A. R. of the District of Columbia, better known as the Drummer Boy of Chickamauga, who became a Union soldier and served throughout the Civil War.

The crowd cheered the ancient warrior as he gave to Lindbergh a scroll from veterans' organizations of the District of Columbia.

"If you want to say a few words," General Fries said to Lindbergh in a low voice, "I know the thousands here will be overjoyed."

MAKES SHORT ADDRESS

The flier looked at the wistful, wasted faces of the men in the wheel chairs. It is doubtful if he saw the tens of thousands beyond the ropes. The famous Lindbergh smile made a white gleam across his face. He stepped to the front of the stand and said:

"Once while I was in France I said I hoped to get somehow, some time, to some place where I wouldn't have to do anything or say anything. I was told that I would soon be back home in America and that I then could do what I pleased. Well, here I am back home and I have to talk more than I did in Europe."

He grinned widely while the crowd roared its laughter and applause.

"A lot has been said about my transatlantic flight. That's all well enough in its way, but it is well not to forget those who during the World War performed deeds of heroism that were overshadowed at the time by the things that went on all around them."

It was plain that his thoughts were with the blinded, shell-shocked, and pain-wrenched men he had seen in their beds on the second floor of the hospital.

"These men," he went on, "did things far more daring than anything that has ever been done in times of peace."

A tremendous burst of approval came in response to this tribute and he waited until it had ended.

His eyes lowered until they rested upon the white forms in the wheel chairs. His voice lowered and deepened as though in prayer.

"This is a fitting time," he said, "for all of us to remember these veterans of the World War."

Abruptly he stopped, turned, and walked to the chair beside his mother.

Here was natural eloquence, a superb sense of the fitness of things. He had struck a chord that brought with it sudden tears to the eyes of many.

WALKS AMONG HELPLESS

After the applause had subsided somewhat, he and his mother walked with General Kennedy from wheel chair to wheel chair and spoke a few words to each broken man.   To Johnny Jackson, of South Carolina, and Tom Cushing, of North Carolina, buddies who lay side by side, he gave the first hearty handclasps. To Ralph Grimm, a veteran of the 89th Division, hailing from Colorado, he spoke a few words.   Both of Grimm's legs have been amputated at the hip but he was as chipper as a lark as he grinned and chatted to Lindbergh.

Young Fred Akin, of Jasper, Georgia, a veteran of the 56th Division, whose right leg has been shattered by gunshot and whose nerves are raging tyrants, forgot all his troubles as Mrs. Lindbergh mothered him for a moment.

Stalwart Jim Haggin, of Gayville, South Dakota, who was wounded terribly while in action with the Fourth Division, received more than his share of attention from both the flier and his mother.

But it was to John L. Connor, of Philadelphia, and his buddy, Tom Cooper, that most of the attention came from Lindbergh.   They were radiant after he had passed.

"He's some kid," said Connor.   "He makes us all proud we're Americans."

They watched him and his mother disappear up the hill, these helpless men in the wheel chairs.   Then they put on the hats and caps they had laid aside by way of salute and the nurses came to wheel them back to their rooms.

CHAPTER XXXIV

NEW YORK'S MIGHTY WELCOME

ON Saturday, June 11, official America through its President and dignitaries of every degree welcomed and honored Colonel Charles Augustus Lindbergh. On the following Monday, all America and all the world, through the tongues and ears and eyes of more than two millions of their representatives, hailed and saw and heard this universal hero and took him to their hearts.

New York, mosaic of every race and every rank, enthroned the rusty-haired and widely grinning flier upon the turned-back top of an automobile, with an enthusiasm that brought back memories of Dewey Day, the Armistice Day jubilation, and the Victory Parade of the American Expeditionary Force returned from the World War. The receptions to the King and Queen of the Belgians, the Prince of Wales, and other distinguished Europeans, or to some of the minor heroes and heroines of the past few years, were simply dimmed to insignificance by the positive worship that the crowds showed for the heroic young man.

In the automobile directly behind him was his radiant mother, and around these two the city framed a volcano of cheering and a carnival of jubilation while it poured upon them from the tall cliffs of lower Broadway a Niagara of ticker tape, confetti, and paper snow.

What a crowd it was and how it enjoyed itself!   The
police estimate said more than two million men, women,
and children were in that tightly packed double-banked
mass of humanity between the Battery and the Mall in
Central Park.   To one who passed with Lindbergh
through that wildly yelling, dangerously surging aisle,
it seemed that the estimate was too low by half.

It was a triumphal procession that far surpassed
any that had ever marched in honor of an individual
in the history of the world, a scene of jubilation only
matched by the delirium of joy that broke all bounds
on Armistice night.

New York had been balked of its keen desire to be
the first to welcome the hero of the first and only transatlantic solo flight.   Some predicted that the disappointment which came with Lindbergh's acceptance
of President Coolidge's invitation to go to Washington
directly would have its effect in a lessening of the
numbers and enthusiasm of the New York reception.

How silly was that forecast was demonstrated when
the Lone Eagle returned to the city from which he
had flown to Paris.   Not another person could have
been jammed between curb and house line, even though
vaseline and a shoehorn had been brought into play.
The maximum of noise and enthusiasm came from
town and river.   Beyond that achievement lay nothing
but hoarseness and delirium.

Through the beauty of the river parade, culminating
in its chorus of shrieking sirens, the swooping down
and droning of files and squadrons of airplanes, the
pomp and frenzy of the parade, the eulogies and decorations of the ceremonies at the City Hall and in the

Mall of the park, young Lindbergh radiated modesty, humor, and a serenity that marks the man of high purpose and character.

He was of that crowd and knew its very heartbeat. No need to interpret him to them. The ready grin— it is inches too wide and jolly for a smile—did all that for him. In him shone the quick psychology of his Congressman-father, who was a famous vote getter, and the easy charm of his school-teacher mother.

How well he knew the millions around him was shown in his talk with newspaper men on the cutter *Macom*, his response to the rough and ready commands of the photographers, his self-possessed address at the City Hall, which was sent by radio over thousands of miles to millions of people, his words in the Mall, and his greetings to the crowd from his casual throne on the back of the automobile.

From 11.58 on that Monday morning, when he made a feather-light landing before 5000 applauding watchers, exactly two hours and four minutes after he had hopped off from Bolling Field, Washington, until he went to bed late at night in the modern apartment of H. H. Frazee, 270 Park Avenue, he had New York at his feet.

THE MAYOR'S PROCLAMATION

By general consent Monday had been turned into a fete day, and the people were in full accord with the Mayor, who had issued a proclamation requesting that the schools be closed on that day, and that the people turn out *en masse* to do honor to the young aviator. Following is the Mayor's proclamation:

CITY OF NEW YORK

OFFICE OF THE MAYOR

PROCLAMATION

The whole world is still echoing with
the acclamation and applause which
greeted Captain Charles A. Lindbergh
when he completed his prodigious voyage
by air from New York to Paris. Seldom
in the history of the world has there been
such a glorious exhibition of courage,
skill, perseverance, and self-reliance by a
single individual. All Europe, thrilled
by the intrepidity of this splendid American youth and electrified by his miraculous achievement, rose spontaneously to
decorate him with the honors and praise
which his single-handed enterprise so
richly merited. His historic accomplishment and the spirit of heroic modesty in
which he has worn his laurels have been
powerful influences in promoting among
European peoples a strong feeling of good
will and sympathetic appreciation for
America and Americans.

On June 13 Captain Lindbergh returns
to the City of New York, the city from
which he ascended on his triumphant
flight. The officials of the city and its
unanimous population are eager to welcome him with traditional metropolitan
sincerity and enthusiasm.

I therefore proclaim June 13, 1927, as a day of public celebration in the City of New York.   I recommend that the schools of our city be closed on that day for the purpose of impressing on the minds of our children the great lesson to be derived from the courage, the faith, the sacrifice, and the patriotism which characterized Captain Lindbergh's wonderful exploit.

I request that the national colors be displayed from every public and private building and I urge that the business men of our city coöperate in so far as convenient in proclaiming the welcome of New York City to our distinguished and heroic guest.

Given under my hand and seal of the City of New York this day, June 9, 1927.

JAMES J. WALKER.

By the Mayor:

EDWARD L. STANTON, Secretary to the Mayor.

THE ARRIVAL IN NEW YORK

It had been planned at first that Colonel Lindbergh should fly in an amphibian plane from Washington to the waters of New York Bay, there to meet the official welcoming boat, *Macom*.   But the Lone Eagle did not want to be separated from his own plane, and he proposed to fly in the *Spirit of St. Louis*.

As matters turned out, it would have been better had the plans stood as at first announced, since the *Spirit of St. Louis* developed a jammed valve in the morning's tests. It was too late then to dig up an amphibian, so Lindbergh leaped into a black and yellow Army Hornet single-seater and jumped off for Mitchell Field.

He found the pipeline to the main tank of gasoline clogged, promptly turned on the line to the emergency tank and made the hop on that supply. Thirty pursuit planes composed his escort of honor from Bolling Field and these were met with another squadron of honor as he approached Mitchell Field.

Captain Ira C. Eaker was waiting at the stick of an amphibian. Before the crowd that had guessed the "secret landing field" could surround and hamper his movements, the flier leaped into a waiting automobile and was whisked down the field, which lies only a mile away from the runway from which he made his running jump to Europe. When the five thousand had been completely taken aback by the maneuver of the speeding motor, he was rushed back to the amphibian and was again in the air four minutes after reaching the airdrome.

It was only a short hop to New York Bay, where the *Macom*, with the big reception committee, headed by Grover A. Whalen, was waiting. In a jiffy he was aboard and reporters and photographers were at him. He told of the trouble with his beloved *Spirit of St. Louis*.

"Some sea water got into the valve and a jam resulted," he explained. "We didn't find the trouble until this morning."

"Will you fly back to Washington for it before going to St. Louis or will someone fly it to New York for you?"

"I haven't decided about that. No one has ever flown that ship except me. We will have to think over what is to be done. I expect it to be all right in a day or so."

"Did you make the flight to Paris solely to get the Orteig prize of $25,000?"

"No. The offer of the prize was a challenge to aviators and that was one reason I flew. I also went to further aëronautics generally."

"Didn't you take a big chance at your start for Paris from Roosevelt Field when you flew so near the network of telephone wires?"

"There wasn't much of a chance. I measured the distance between the ship and the wires with my eyes. I cleared them by about twenty feet."

The photographers demanded their share of him and got it. The *Macom* was now in the lane of more than two hundred river craft of all descriptions, the lines beginning at Wadsworth Island and extending up the bay toward the Battery. Flags were fluttering from every mast and staff and sirens were shrieking like wailing demons. Shepherded by Whalen, the flier was escorted to the bridge of the *Macom* to acknowledge the wildest salutes ever heard in the harbor.

At the Battery Graham McNamee had been telling millions of radio listeners-in of the Colonel's approach. More than ten thousand soldiers and sailors, both active and veterans of past wars, had passed up Broadway past the reviewing stand at City Hall and were waiting to place the hero at their head just beyond that point.

As he came off the gangplank, McNamee grabbed him for a brief "Hello, New York," into the microphone. A gorgeously decorated limousine was waiting for him and Whalen. He was at once initiated in the proper manner to take a typical New York welcome. With a flashing grin, he accepted the suggestion and perched himself upon the folded-back top of the car with his feet resting on the seat. Hatless, bowing to right and left, he was in sharp contrast to the silk-hatted, serious-faced personages in front of him.

In the second car was one who fairly shared the honors of the day with him. Everybody recognized the radiant mother whose smile has become known to millions.

The procession to her was one long thrill. Her eyes were fixed with shining intentness upon the car ahead and the tall, lean, young figure on its jolting throne.

LIKE A TORRENTIAL UPROAR

That bedlam of the lower Broadway canyon still rings in ears that heard it. It was a sustained, high-pitched shriek with pulsing rhythms like the staccato stutterings of a world-shaking riveting machine. In it were yips of tight-throated boys who saw in the tanned Lindbergh a model for their lives. Here was the deep baying of men calling over and over, "Lindbergh! Lindbergh!"

Overlying the torrential uproar like spindrift on a mighty wave was the piercing soprano of countless women who called with sobbing catches in their throats.

Many of the older of these women had brought their children to see this youth and the mother who is his best girl. Some of these were youngsters of less than ten. Some carried mere babies in their arms.

"What do you think of a woman who would take a little child into a crowd like this?" demanded Phillip Carlin, one of the broadcasters, from his perch on the roof of City Hall. "She must be insane."

"Well, I dunno," mused a big sergeant of police as he pressed men back from one little group of a mother and two children. "I think all the children of America ought to be here today to see this mother and this son and to realize what they stand for. It would be a mighty good thing for the future of this country, so it would."

But it was a dangerous place for children and for grown-ups as well. In that terrific jam between the Battery and City Hall many persons panic-stricken and in the clutches of that hysteria known as claustrophobia, which attacks those caught in crowds, shrieked and fainted. Sudden maddened rushes sent portions of the crowd surging against the ropes.

The New York police individually and as a whole performed magnificently in these emergencies. The bulges in the jam were relieved by taking the bulkiest men at the apex of the rushes and pulling them under the ropes into the streets.

In some cases these persons were the cause of the surging. In others, they were merely innocent wedges of the immense mass behind them. Some of the men lost collars and portions of their coats when they were yanked out of the press, but no one was hurt except in his dignity. These tactics had immediate psychological results. Those near by dreaded the same handling for themselves and shrank back from the ropes, carrying their neighbors with them.

During all this excitement, the police used only their hands. No one carried a club. Once when a large section of the crowd between Ann and Fulton Streets threatened to break the ropes and hurl itself into the line of march, fifty reserve bluecoats with drawn night sticks came up on the double quick. The mere sight of their chilled-steel efficiency set the crowd back on its heels and no more trouble came in that quarter.

As Lindbergh's slow progress up to the City Hall held him for a minute at a time before a part of the crowd, girls attempted to throw flowers into his lap and thousands blew kisses toward him. If he saw any of these advances he gave no sign. Occasionally he waved his now famous gray felt hat with the wide black band. More often he just bowed and grinned.

RECEPTION BY THE MAYOR

The weariness that lay like a gray shade over his face yesterday after two days of terrific heat and nerve-exhausting receptions in Washington had almost disappeared. His color was about normal, his keen, blue eyes were merry and clear and his voice deep and under control. When he looked squintingly aloft to the windows of the tall buildings from which came tape and torn bits of paper like snow sparkling in the sunlight, his lips puckered in an involuntary whistle.

As his automobile turned at City Hall into the avenue made by the reviewing stands for whose seats the whole town had been madly scrambling for weeks, the din was redoubled. Buglers on the steps of City

Hall sang, "See, the Conquering Hero Comes," with golden-throated brilliance. Mayor James J. Walker came with outstretched hands to greet him and led him to the front of the platform before a double-faced microphone.

The Mayor's address of welcome was one of his wittiest and most eloquent. Lindbergh, remembering his gallant and independent-minded father, straightened, flushed, and nodded emphatically when the Mayor declared that as chief executive of the world's foremost city, he as a son of an immigrant was proud to acclaim and to welcome the son of another immigrant.

Throughout that address and the brief words of Grover A. Whalen, Lindbergh stood smiling, the tallest and gayest figure on the platform. When he stepped to the microphone to respond it seemed that the whole world of mad sound had suddenly become mute.

In its essentials, his address expressed the same thoughts to which he had given utterance in his talk Saturday night before the National Press Club of Washington and its guests. One difference was his exhortation to the American people that it must not expect quick results from aviation. He said that regular transatlantic passenger airplane service must wait upon seadromes placed on the ocean, further experimentation in airplane development, multimotored ships, and scientific tests generally. Perhaps in five or ten years, he predicted, transatlantic service may be a fact which will not excite comment. His cool, reasonable words were evidence how widely they missed the mark who dubbed him the "flying fool."

"Let me dispense with an unnecessary function,"

Mayor Walker said in presenting the scroll, "by telling you that if you have prepared yourself with any letters of introduction to New York they are not necessary.

"You are a great grammarian, you have given added definition to the word 'we.' We are familiar with the editorial 'we,' but not until you arrived in Paris were we aware of the aëronautical 'we.' You have given to the world a flying pronoun.

"That word was a vindication of the courage and the hopes of Nungesser and Coli, who live now only in the memory of the peoples of the world.

"New York City is yours. I don't give it to you. You have won it. I congratulate you and welcome you into the world city, that you may look the world in the face."

LINDBERGH REPLIES

In a few sentences Lindbergh told of his receptions in Europe.

"When I was preparing to leave for Europe," he said, "I was told that if we landed in Le Bourget we might expect a rather demonstrative reception. After one-half hour at Le Bourget, I didn't believe anyone in New York would have the slightest idea of the reception given us.

"And again at Brussels and also at London. Why, in London 1500 of the pride of Scotland Yard were lost in a crowd at Croydon as completely as though they had been dropped in the ocean. Except around the car in which I was and around the plane, I don't recall ever seeing two of them together.

"At Washington there was another enormous reception, but at New York I believe that there was a reception greater than all four put together. I wonder what those London bobbies would have thought of their position here.

"When I landed at Le Bourget I landed looking forward to the pleasure of seeing Europe and the British Isles. I learned to speak of Europe and the British Isles after I landed in London. I had been away from America a little less than two days. I have been greatly interested in the things I saw while passing over southern England and France, and I was not in any hurry to get back home.

"By the time I had spent about a week in France and a short time in Belgium and England, and had opened a few cables from the United States, I found that I did not have much to say about how long I would stay over there. The Ambassador in London said that it was not an order to go back home, but there would be a battleship waiting in a few days.

"So I left Europe and the British Isles with the regret that I had been unable to see either Europe or the British Isles. When I started up the Potomac from the *Memphis* I decided that I was not so sorry that I had taken the Ambassador's advice. After spending about an hour in New York I know I am not.

"In regard to aviation, I would like to say just a few words; that is, not to expect too rapid development. We are not going to have transatlantic service in a few months. We will have it eventually; it is inevitable, but it will be after careful development and experimental research. We should have it probably within five or ten years; but any attempt to fly across

the Atlantic regularly without multimotors, without
stations at intervals along the route, and without a
flying boat that can weather some storm would be
foolhardy. I want you to remember that aviation
has developed on a sound basis, and it will continue
to develop on a sound basis.

"I thank you."

The end of his speech came with characteristic
abruptness. Lindbergh believes in finishing when
his thoughts are at an end. He doesn't spin fine words
into artistic perorations. When he concludes whatever he has on his mind, he says "I thank you," turns
quickly on his heel and takes his chair. That "I thank
you" is as clean cut as the swing of a razor. Crowds
have come to look for it and apparently they love it.

GREETED BY THE GOVERNOR

No Cæsar, Pompey, Napoleon, or other conqueror
ever received the ovation upon his return from
successful wars that overwhelmed this young, peaceful
son of the Vikings on his progress up Fifth Avenue to
the Mall in Central Park. School children free on a
holiday, brokers and their clerks taking advantage of
the shut-down in Wall Street in honor of the hero,
business and professional men and their employees who
found that business could not be transacted when New
York was Lindbergh-mad, were in that tremendous
crush. Reviewing stands along the noble thorough-
fare were jammed with leaders of the social, business,
and financial worlds. These were as eager in their
cheering as the most excited schoolboys. To them,
the lad with his feet on the back seat of the big auto-

mobile represented the peak of individuality, the soul that took the ultimate chance alone.

In the Mall, Governor Alfred E. Smith awaited with the Medal of Valor of New York State to pin beside the Medal of Valor of New York City that had been placed there by Mayor Walker.

The Governor was in fine fettle. That he is both wise and witty was demonstrated when, seeing the utter exhaustion of nerves in Lindbergh's features, he tactfully cut his planned address to a fraction of his original intention. It was in the Mall that this exhaustion became for the first time apparent.

The strain of the long day with its hitches and hazards had told at last. One can't get up before six o'clock in the morning, attend a big breakfast of honor, motor to a flying field, tinker with a balky plane, take a strange ship, find its gas line out of kelter, fly it on the emergency line more than two hours, and on top of these nerve-tolltakers undergo the tests of interviews, speeches, and the most tremendous demonstration of his life without paying dearly for all of these experiences.

Al Smith never did a kinder deed nor one in which his quick, human understanding stood him in good stead than when he mercifully cut short those ceremonies in the Mall.

In presenting the Medal of Valor, Governor Smith commented on the inscription:

"Awarded," he read, "to Captain—you can have that changed to Colonel—Lindbergh, because I understand you are a colonel now. And I hope you will be a general."

Colonel Lindbergh, replying, said:

"I am greatly pleased to see the French flag, because less than two weeks ago I saw the Stars and Stripes in the same way among the flags of France. America has a true friend in France."

NEW YORK'S SCROLL TO LINDBERGH

The scroll which Mayor Walker, on behalf of the citizens of New York, presented to Colonel Lindbergh, on June 13, 1927, read as follows:

The City of New York to Colonel Charles A. Lindbergh, America's Air Ambassador, New York to Paris Non-stop Flight, Greeting:

On this historic spot and in this historic seat of our city government it has been our custom to extend our municipal welcome to many of the notable people of the world.

Here the chief magistrates of the City of New York have received many noted heroes of the land, the sea and air. Kings and leaders of mankind, the highest dignitaries of Church and State and heroes in the many fields of human endeavor have here received the hearty and cordial official welcome which always marks the hospitality of the City of New York.

Today we equal the height and dignity of all the traditions that through the years has been established here, as on behalf of the millions of New York citizens who have been thrilled and inspired

by your heroic deed, I welcome you—
Colonel Charles A. Lindbergh—back to
the city from which you set forth in your
courageous nonstop flight to Paris.

From this, the youngest of the great
cities of the earth, your intrepid voyage
carried you, braving the perils of the air
and the sea, to Paris, one of the oldest
cities of the world, and by your glorious
flight you not only attained the ambition
of aëronautic science, but, enhancing your
prodigious accomplishment by the modesty and diplomacy that is found only in
genuine heroism, you inspired in the
hearts of European peoples a warmer
affection and a greater admiration for
your own beloved country and her people.

The youth of our Nation has found in
your conquering spirit of courage and
youth an encouraging and illustrious
example.

The great fame which you have won
in the glory of your youth, not only for
yourself but for America, this city inevi-
tably shares with you.   From New York
you sailed on your adventurous exploit;
to New York you return bearing the triumphant laurels of the whole world's
tribute, and the name of our fair city is
linked forever with the fame that is yours.

The people of New York delight to
honor you; their hearts are wide open to

you, and, in their name, I present to you
this (scroll of honored welcome) that you
may have a permanent record of how the
people of New York, speaking through
me, hold you and your epoch-making
deed in honor for all time.

PHILADELPHIA SHOUTS GREETINGS TO THE SKY

An hour or two before New York's great welcome,
Philadelphia, at a mere glimpse of the Conqueror of
the Atlantic, as he sped over the city from Washington,
literally howled itself speechless.

By faith, Philadelphia gave its whole-hearted greeting to "Slim" Lindbergh. It could not see him. It
saw only a birdman skimming over the famous Penn
Tower and over the skyscrapers and over the Delaware
River, with a squadron of other birdmen accompanying
him.

Denied the privilege of acclaiming the Lone Eagle
on terra firma, the people flung their applause to the
wide sky as he swept on with his escort.

He was scheduled to arrive at 10.30 in the morning,
but long before that time Philadelphia was "on
tiptoe."

In the streets, at the windows, on the housetops, the
people scanned the heavens, till the roar went up,
"Here he comes! Lindbergh! Lindbergh!"

Business had been suspended that morning in "the
Workshop of the World." Little was talked of except
that Captain—now Colonel—Lindbergh was on his
way from Washington, and that he was to fly over
Philadelphia. Crowds gathered on the new Delaware

River Bridge; in the open spaces; on places of vantage where a nearly unobstructed view of the flying hero might be obtained, and where he might be kept in sight as long as possible.

On the tallest skyscrapers and on the roofs of the lowliest homes the citizens were clustered. Some even took up precarious positions on the sloping roofs of water tanks on the high buildings, as if to be nearer the plane carrying the young aviator.

It was a short time after eleven o'clock that those who waited in the southeastern section of the city caught the first glimpse of planes in the southern sky. No radio or telegraph could have sped the news more swiftly. As the fleet ships of the air, speeding onward in flights of three, with Lindbergh in the van, roared overhead, the whistles of factories and of ships in the river began their frantic diapason. Others joined in, and then human voices took up the chorus.

There were no grandstands; no formal reception; no silk hats; no bands. But there was a mighty welcome, an unorganized but wildly clamorous welcome, a people's welcome, heartfelt and spontaneous. It was a chorus from two million throats that defied the space intervening between the Lone Eagle and the multitudes.

In the fifteen minutes which it required Colonel Lindbergh and his escort of twenty-one planes to appear from the south and disappear into the north, Philadelphia left no room for doubt of its enthusiasm.

WESTWARD AND HOMEWARD

There were more gala days to follow in New York. But while the Lone Eagle appreciated the welcomes of the East, as he had appreciated the welcomes of Europe, he was eager to get in touch with that other part of himself—the famous "we," which, as all the world now knows, means Lindbergh and the *Spirit of St. Louis*—and wing his way westward and homeward.

The city of St. Louis awaited him—impatiently. It was St. Louis that backed him; St. Louis that had faith in his venture when, little known to others, he hopped off to New York, and from there to Paris—and fame!

Amazing names had been given him: "Lone Eagle," "Columbus of the Air," "Ace of the Atlantic," "Knight of the Air," "Flying Viking," "Conqueror of the Atlantic," "Galahad of the Air"—but it was as "Slim" Lindbergh the people of St. Louis had remembered the intrepid flier, and impatiently they awaited him, eager to give him a welcome which in heartiness and pride would outshine all other welcomes, wonderful as they had been.

In the midst of all the acclaim Colonel Lindbergh retained his poise, his quiet demeanor. Feted by kings, idolized by uncounted multitudes, he had returned unspoiled.

It is not too much to say that this incredible boy from the West has served America in many unique capacities: as an exemplar, as an inspirer, as a complete educational system in himself, as a challenge, as an "Ambassador" and as an achiever.

* 288 pp. + 32 pp. ill.